PRAISE FOR *LOCAL LEGENDS*

'*Local Legends* is a must-read for anyone in local government in Australia, New Zealand – or elsewhere for that matter. It offers evidence-based insight leading logically to a what-to-do-next opinion. A masterful work, engagingly written, by someone from local government who clearly wants to deliver better outcomes for Councils and residents. Congratulations Alicia, *Local Legends* is a book that will make a difference to the way people live. Any chance you could turn your mind to defence, inflation, and housing?'

Bernard Salt AM, Founder of the Demographics Group

'*Local Legends* is a masterclass in strategic leadership for local government. With sharp insights and practical advice, it shines a light on the often-underappreciated role of local councils and shows how they can drive social progress. Alicia's engaging style and real-world examples make complex concepts fun, accessible, and actionable. It's a must-read for anyone passionate about making a long-term impact and leaving a lasting legacy in their community.'

Paul Evans, Independent Director

'This book is a highly approachable and engaging touchstone for local government managers (appointed and elected) that is subtly but profoundly grounded in local public administration thinking (public value creation, strategic management, decision-making theory, organisational design) informed by years of experience. Local government managers will find it reassuring, revelatory and – most importantly – *useful* for continually improving their practice across the range of skills required for being a successful local government leader.'

Dr Bligh Grant, Adjunct Associate Professor, University of Technology Sydney

'Never before have I read anything that so perfectly articulates how hard and rewarding local government can be! Local government demands resilience in the face of challenges and rewards with the profound joy of seeing a community thrive. For those who seek to understand and contribute to this vital sphere, *Local Legends* offers a comprehensive playbook that balances the difficulties with the undeniable rewards of public service.'

Clinton Jury, CEO, Local Government Association of South Australia

'*Local Legends* is an insightful look under the lid of local government. Meticulously well researched, this book combines Alicia's passion for local government with her first-hand experience inside the tent. This backdrop, coupled with years of supporting local authorities and executives finding their way through the endless complexities this sector struggles with, provides anyone with more than a passing interest in the machinery behind local communities something to think about – there is some real wisdom found within these pages. This "how-to guide" for those in the sector should not go unnoticed.'

Dr Haydn Read, Te Hēteri, Te Whānau-ā-Apanui; Visiting Scholar, University of Ottawa

LOCAL LEGENDS

LOCAL LEGENDS

HOW TO MAKE A DIFFERENCE IN LOCAL GOVERNMENT

Alicia McKay

ISBN: 978-1-923225-10-7

Book production and text design by Publish Central
Cover design by Pipeline Design

The paper this book is printed on is certified as environmentally friendly.

Contents

Introduction

My first job out of university was at a Council in a little town in the South Island of New Zealand. I had no idea what I was heading into. After completing a four-year politics degree, I knew more about the Cold War than what happened in a Council. Local government had hardly been mentioned.

This is the attention and respect local government generally receives, even among political boffins. Local government is broadly under-appreciated, even in the public sector. It has no constitutional recognition in Australia and is the least funded arm of government in both Australia and New Zealand. Many people don't know what their Council does.

For the first few months of that job, I walked around in a delighted haze as I came to grips with the daily reality of local democracy. People could speak directly to their elected members about issues that mattered to them – and the Council legally had to consider those views? Athenian direct-democracy style? I was blown away. I still am.

I left that job four years later but never left local government. In the last decade, I've worked with more than 50 different Councils across Australia and New Zealand, several local government associations and industry peak bodies, and dozens of sector-adjacent companies and government departments in planning, community development, infrastructure, transport, and the environment. I cannot seem to stay away.

If you work in local government, you'll know why. It burrows into your heart – the community connection, the tangible impact, the genuine people. The (many!) frustrations can't keep us away for long.

I'm passionate about the difference local government can and does make in communities. When the world is tilted on its axis, public trust in politics and the media is justifiably dicey, and people are increasingly disconnected from civic society and one another, I firmly believe local government is more important than ever.

THE PUBLIC SECTOR UNDERDOG

Local government is underfunded and misunderstood. Councils are the poor cousins of the public sector, a periodic scapegoat for public spending gone awry, and the closest access point for anyone annoyed with government services.

I could write an entire book arguing local government should be more respected, enjoy more legal protection, and be better funded and empowered. It would be a good use of my time and a worthy read. Thankfully, many experts have already done this work.

In New Zealand, the 2023 Future for Local Government report[1] highlighted the critical role of local government in managing – among other things – extreme weather events, pandemic recovery, global conflict, economic inequity, and low social cohesion. The

---

1   Future for Local Government Review Panel, 2023.

panel bluntly described the sector's constraints and the corrosive effect of sustained underinvestment from higher tiers of government. They endorse what experts have recommended for decades: mandate certainty, sustainable funding, and greater democratic empowerment.

This review is unlikely to provoke meaningful action. Thoughtful analyses of systemic barriers to local government performance rarely do. Governments prefer to act on reports that suggest cracking the whip, like the 2022 Local Government Culture Report in Victoria[2], which targets Councillor misbehaviour and misconduct. Legislative tweaks, regulatory oversight, and general tut-tutting from the government are easy to come by, but structural change is not.

The narrative across states and territories in Australia and regions and districts in New Zealand is disappointingly consistent: Councils are a problem that needs solving.

Councils work within a regime of contradictions. They provide services inside a legislative framework that requires elections, community engagement, and consultative decisions – and are asked why their operations aren't more efficient. They confront increasingly constrained funding environments and watch their share of the total tax take decrease over decades – only for those financial struggles to be used as evidence they're bad with money. They absorb the ongoing transfer of costs, services, and responsibilities from state and non-profit actors – before being accused of scope creep and told to 'get back to basics'. They are mandated to make intergenerational decisions on infrastructure and community facilities – and rebuked for using intergenerational funding mechanisms.

In short, local government is a victim of political gaslighting.

* * *

---

2   PWC, 2022.

In Australia and New Zealand, local government deserves comprehensive reform. Councils require funding arrangements that recognise their complexity, diversity, and impact. They need respect, support, and investment to face the frontline of our most pressing global challenges: social division, climate transition, economic uncertainty, and natural disasters.

Assuming this isn't coming anytime soon, they must act regardless. Councils need all the tools they can get to tackle their challenges, and this book is my contribution to those tools.

> **Local government is a victim of political gaslighting.**

AGENTS OF PROGRESS

If we learned anything during the COVID-19 pandemic, it's that some services are more essential than others. Councils do work that isn't sexy or glamorous; the work that infiltrates our daily lives and that we take for granted (but notice instantly if it fails).

When we quarantined in our homes, local government persisted behind the scenes. As the world went mad, Kiwis and Aussies enjoyed clean drinking water, safe communities, and drivable roads without missing a beat.

Local connections to the community were vital at this time – and are still. Growing social unease and disconnection, accelerating artificial intelligence, and increasing mistrust of media and public institutions threaten social, economic, and environmental progress. We need people on the ground.

Councils are doing more than ever. The responsibilities and costs shifted to local government are increasing – as is the complexity of those requirements – and debates around scope are functionally irrelevant. Whether or not you believe Councils should deal with community challenges and whether or not they are adequately equipped to do so, they *are*. Councils are the first layer of public defence. They face global challenges at the local level. They are at the front line of coastal erosion and weather events and are quickly and tangibly affected by housing insecurity, poverty, and crime.

Making progress in this environment, with increasing expectations and decreasing real-term funding, is difficult. Structural barriers aside, the daily constraints to Councils realising their potential are the same things that make the sector so powerful: tangible impact, personal investment, and local connection. The desire for tangible impact drags leaders into short-term, operational problem-solving. Personal investment creates blind spots and compromises decision quality. Local connection scares leaders away from making courageous choices.

But harnessed, those double-edged swords can be the same forces propelling local government to a leadership position in a world struggling to hold together. Local government is well-positioned to lead the charge on some of the most pressing issues of our day. Local government leaders – elected and employed – can be community visionaries, master collaborators, and focused decision-makers. They can boldly innovate, protect what's unique about their place, and lead the charge toward fairer, safer, healthier communities for current and future generations.

In this book, I make the case that:

- Local government is an agent of social progress with unique capabilities and untapped potential to create long-term public value.
- Realising this potential will require strategic leadership from elected members and executive managers.

▌ The three most effective interventions for Councils are a bigger-picture perspective, productive relationships within and between governance and management, and more strategic decisions.

Who this book is for

I love local government. I love working with Councillors, managers, and officers to support their work – work that is special, important, and hard. This book is a labour of that love.

Local Legends is a guide for Councillors and Council managers, whom I will collectively refer to as 'local government leaders'.

This book will help local government leaders who are:

▌ Defensive and frustrated by staff and Councillor interactions.

▌ Discouraged by strategies and plans that go nowhere.

▌ Overwhelmed by never-ending reports and meetings.

▌ Caught in a reactive cycle of daily drama.

▌ Struggling to build shared purpose and ownership.

I will explore the reasons for those challenges and present suggestions for Councils to move forward despite, or even because of, their uniquely tricky environment.

WE NEED STRATEGIC LOCAL LEADERS

In this book, elected members and executive managers will learn to become more strategic leaders and exponentially increase the value you generate for your community. You will learn the key shifts needed to leave a legacy and make good decisions.

This is work worth doing. Strategic thinking, planning, and decisions can shift the trajectory of your Council and community.

The data (and my professional experience) suggests it will deliver many benefits.[3]

If you're a local government leader, strategic, big-picture leadership *is your job*. Others have been hired to handle operational issues, and they know better than you. Service delivery is their core responsibility. Direction-setting and decision-making are yours.

If you're a Councillor, you've been elected to be strategic. If you are a senior manager, you've been hired for the same. Your job is no more or less important than anyone else's, but *it is your job,* and chances are you've had little guidance on how to be the strategic leader your Council and community needs.

This book hopes to bridge that gap. If you want to do work that matters in a complex world, thinking and acting strategically is more important than ever. If it is time for you to take the reins as the strategic local legend your community needs, this book is for you.

---

3   A meta-analysis of over 9000 public sector organisations has proven that strategic planning improves organisational performance. On average, it has a positive impact. This impact accelerates when performance is measured as 'an organization's ability to achieve its goals.' George et al., 2019. In short: strategy won't necessarily make you more efficient, but it will make you more effective.

01

Eiffel Tower leadership

'We have come, writers, painters, sculptors, architects,
passionate enthusiasts of the hitherto untouched beauty of
Paris, to protest with all our strength, all our indignation,
in the name of the unknown French taste, in the name of art
and of French history threatened, against the erection, in the
heart of our capital, of the useless and monstrous Eiffel Tower,
which public malignity, often marked by common sense and
the spirit of justice, has already named of "Tower of Babel".'

'Protest Against the Tower of Monsieur Eiffel'
Le Temps newspaper, 14 February 1878

The City of Paris has owned the Eiffel Tower since its construction in 1889. Engineer Gustave Eiffel built the tower for the Exposition Universelle, a world's fair, after narrowly beating architect rival Jules Bourdais' 1200-foot granite Sun Tower in a design competition. Today, the tower is a global icon, synonymous with Paris's romance and allure. It attracts over seven million visitors every year.

It's a decision that's aged well – but the people of Paris were not universally pleased with the tower's construction. Writers and artists were initially scornful of the design and warned it was so tacky even America would reject it (ha!). The pressure on the Council to change tack was high, including from the 40 or so famous names who signed the 'Protest Against the Tower of Monsieur Eiffel' in *Le Temps* newspaper, featuring writers and artists such as Guy de Maupassant and Alexandre Dumas. Guy de Maupassant scorned the tower as a 'giant ungainly skeleton … aborting to form a ridiculous, skinny, factory chimney stack'.[4]

Aesthetics aside, the community had safety concerns, too. Neighbouring Champ de Mars residents were so worried about their homes' safety during the tower's construction that a Paris City Council member lodged a lawsuit against Gustave Eiffel on their behalf. In response, Eiffel agreed to be held personally liable for any damage or loss of life during construction. Things were tense.

Almost immediately after its completion, the tide of public opinion turned. Parisians proudly embraced their striking monument as the world flocked to see it. Over 100 years later, in 2012, the Eiffel Tower was declared the world's most valuable monument, worth an estimated 435 billion Euros – six times the value of the closest runner-up, Rome's Colosseum.[5]

Big, bold decisions and long-term legacies often result from a few brave leaders willing to be temporarily unpopular in service of a bigger vision. If that impassioned letter to the paper had swayed the Council, we might not have the Eiffel Tower.

***

---

4   Tour Eiffel, 2023. Amusingly, de Maupassant was said to often lunch on the tower's first floor because it was the only place in the city where he would not see it.

5   Samuel, 2012.

Local government needs more Eiffel Tower leadership – big dreams, bold thinking, and short-term resilience to public pushback for long-term gain.

LEAVE A LEGACY

> 'A real leader is somebody who can help us overcome the limitations of our own individual laziness and selfishness and weakness and fear and get us to do better things than we can get ourselves to do on our own.'
>
> David Foster Wallace

People can be selfish, short-sighted creatures. As individuals, we are myopic, biased, and busy. We think everyone sees the world like we do. We don't have all the information, we can't see the full system and how it fits together, and we have little understanding of long-term consequences. That's why we elect people to make important decisions on our behalf.

Local government leaders are the better angels of our nature. They represent the wider community's needs, consider long-term, systemic consequences, and make choices in the best interests of everyone, even if they're not in the specific interests of anyone. Or so we hope.

Local government leaders are the better angels of our nature.

This is a lot to ask of a civically minded local who suddenly finds herself at the reins of a complex and diverse multi-million-dollar institution – usually for low pay and in part-time hours. Plato's Philosopher Kings were benevolent, knowledgeable sages who trained all their lives to make wise decisions with bold foresight. Modern-day Councillors are more likely to be exhausted business owners juggling an evening meeting schedule with family responsibilities, trying to keep up with detailed technical reports and being lambasted on Facebook for the state of the footpaths.

It's a lot to ask, but local government leadership is more import-ant than ever. In an age of climate change, persistent inequity, and widespread disinformation, we need bold, decisive, values-based leadership. We need local government leaders who, like the City of Paris, envision a brighter future, believe deeply in their place's potential, and stay above the fray. We need leaders to make the right decisions, even when we disagree with them. We need you to be better than us.

Councils provide critical community infrastructure

'There are two kinds of people: those who do the work and those who take the credit. Try to be in the first group; there is less competition there.'

Indira Gandhi

Councils provide critical community infrastructure, but it's not all roads, rates, and rubbish. Sometimes, it's an Eiffel Tower. Sometimes, it's economic infrastructure that enables local businesses to compete nationally or globally. Or tourism infrastructure that attracts visi-tors and creates vibrant towns and cities. Or social infrastructure that supports civic engagement and encourages neighbourhood connections. Or environmental infrastructure that keeps the com-munity healthy and habitable by reducing waste, energy use, and air pollution.

Councils don't just deliver today's services; they create the conditions for tomorrow's success. Eiffel Tower leadership is possible when you know your place so well and care about it so much that you enable your community to succeed beyond its wildest aspirations.

It's inspiring. It's a hell of a mandate. But it isn't easy. Councils are under-resourced, underappreciated, and overstretched. In Australia, Councils deliver almost a quarter of public services for less than 4% of total tax revenue.[6] It's like being the hardest-working employee – when you make yourself indispensable, you're rewarded with more work. For local government, that means more responsibilities transferred from higher government – usually without the revenue or support to deliver them.

> **Councils don't just deliver today's services; they create the conditions for tomorrow's success.**

Local government leadership has the unique potential to contribute to intergenerational change and progress. Leading well in local government can change outcomes for current and future generations. But whether you're on the political or administrative side of the table, this job is harder than people give credit for.

STRATEGY IS THE WAY

This is where strategy comes in. Strategy is the ultimate leveller. When you have big goals and scarce resources, strategy makes the most of the hand you've been dealt.

With strategy, we have a chance. I have spent my career – and life – studying, practising, designing, facilitating, and implementing

---

6   SGS Economics and Planning, 2022.

strategy in organisations of all shapes and sizes. I have only become more enamoured of strategy's transformative potential with time.

When you're clear on where you're going and focused with how to get there, you can achieve the future you want. Strategy will guide your decisions, align people and resources, and take others with you.

When I talk about strategy, I don't mean corporate jargon or glossy documents. Strategy is not a corporate invention; it has existed for millennia. Originally the domain of war generals, strategy has always been necessary for anyone with bold aspirations and limited resources.[7] Strategy is 'something people do', not 'something organisations have.'[8] You actively create strategy with your intentions, values, skills, people, relationships, conversations, experiments, environments, systems, and choices. With strategy, we use our limited time and money cleverly – something local government needs to do, whether they like it or not. As Sir Ernest Rutherford famously remarked: 'We haven't got the money, so we'll have to think'.

Most people have never learned how strategy works, but you're about to.

Strategy 101

Strategy is the *approach* we *choose* to pursue our *goals*.

Approach, because strategy isn't about mapping the steps we'll take (that's a plan). When our strategy is clear, it provides criteria we can use to make good decisions.

Choose, because strategy implies trade-offs. We wouldn't need a strategy if we could do everything we wanted.

Goals, because we don't need a strategy to stay the same. Strategy is synonymous with change.

---

7   Gaddis, J. L., 2018.
8   Vandersmissen & George, 2023.

The three levels of strategy

The model below outlines the three levels of strategy.

The Strategy 101 model

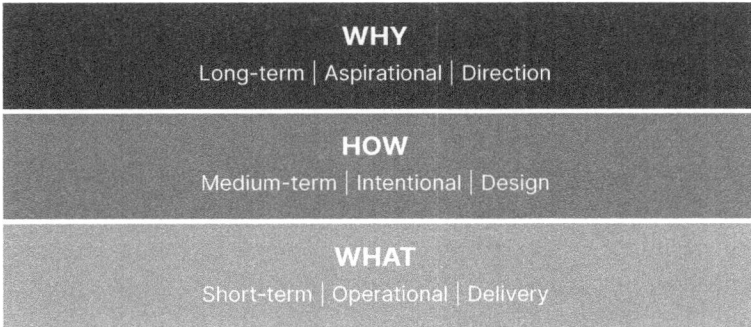

WHY
Long-term | Aspirational | Direction
HOW
Medium-term | Intentional | Design
WHAT
Short-term | Operational | Delivery

The 'why' level

The top of the diagram is the 'why' level, where you find jargon like purpose, vision, and mission. These are our aspirational long-term outcomes: the difference we want to make in the world. When we're clear on our direction, we can choose our path to get there. The 'why' level should rarely change.

The 'how' level

In the middle, the 'how' level is the guts of strategy, where you find jargon like objectives, priorities, and principles. This is where we sharpen our medium-term focus. For most organisations, the 'how' level changes every three to five years.

The 'what' level

The bottom is the 'what' level, which is about planning, actions, and initiatives. These are the operational choices made in the short term: the daily proof of our commitment to long-term aspirations. The 'what' level changes daily, as it should.

The often-missing middle

Most organisations and leaders are comfortable with 'why' and 'what'. They understand the broader vision, and they're overflowing with projects and initiatives. But things become more complicated with 'how'. This is the essence of strategy: the often-missing middle, the connecting piece that brings together our aspirations and operations.

Done well, the *'how'* becomes a filter for action and decisions. Clear medium-term priorities align aspirations with resources.

The 'how' requires trade-offs about using finite resources and attention. This is hard to do – especially in Councils. In local government, trade-offs aren't about reducing the marketing budget or slowing the development of a new product. It could mean letting down a worthy cause or watching conditions worsen.

In an ideal strategy landscape, the three levels will narrow to an inverted triangle. The focused criteria of 'how' narrows the choices available at 'what' – who to hire, which projects to fund, which relationships to build, and what to put first – into a razor-sharp point. But in local government, I often see the opposite. 'Strategic objectives', which should function as narrowing forces, are instead an ever-expanding wish list of community niceties. This explodes the 'what' level of the strategy with limitless possibilities.

Strategy: ideal vs reality

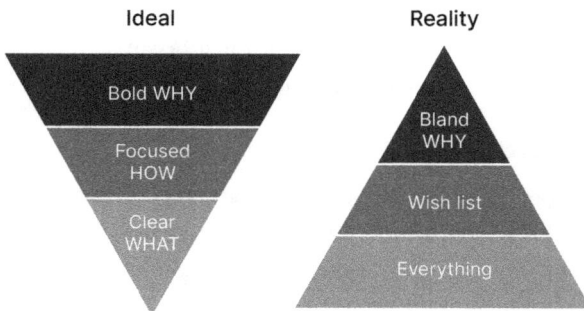

Ideal

Bold WHY
Focused HOW
Clear WHAT

Reality

Bland WHY
Wish list
Everything

Public vs private sector strategy

The Strategy 101 model applies equally to the private and public sectors but plays out differently in each. If you hear someone say, 'You'd never run a business like this!' about the Council, you can use the following explanation to agree with them and explain why.

Private vs public sector

Private sector		Public sector
Profit	**WHY**	Public value
Competition	**HOW**	Collaboration
Tangible	**WHAT**	Intangible

Profit vs public value

The private sector's 'why' is to capture private value for shareholders as profit. But in the public sector, government actors and agencies aim to create *public value*.

For example, a Council running business support programmes creates local economic value. This value is captured by local business owners (profits), residents and visitors (goods, services, and employment) and other tiers of government (increased taxes). The Council receives no financial return or quantifiable benefit.

In this way, local government creates value – and most or all of it is captured by others. That is public value.

Competition vs collaboration

In the private sector, the 'how' is where businesses differentiate for competitive advantage through design, pricing, quality, features, and branding. In the public sector, there is no competition. The government has a functional monopoly on libraries, roads, bridges, etc.

Local government is powered by *collaboration*, not *competition*. Decisions consider diverse inputs and values; the most important choices must have explicit stakeholder and community endorsement. Nothing happens alone, and little happens quickly.

Tangible vs intangible

In the private sector, businesses serve intentionally niche markets. They provide *tangible* products and services that people willingly purchase.

The public sector serves the collective – and not just with tangible goods and services. A Council's *intangible* deliverables include ideas (strategies, initiatives) and rules (policies, regulations, planning guidelines). Some projects and initiatives don't pay dividends for years or decades, and some may never. Plus, citizens can't opt out.

* * *

These factors make it unhelpful to compare Councils with businesses. You'd never run a business this way – nor should you. We're not optimising for the same outcomes. Councils are in the 'business' of long-term public value creation and their strategies reflect their best theories on delivering that value to diverse and unique communities.

Your goals are bigger and more challenging than business

It would be easier if this were a book about strategy in the private sector. 'If you follow my advice, you'll make more money' is a more commercial publishing proposition than 'If you follow my advice, you might make a difference a long time from now, and no one will appreciate it or attribute it to you'.

But, like everything concerning local government, your goals are complicated. Councils don't want something mediocre like money; business is simple in comparison. You're aiming for big, important, earth-shattering, world-changing outcomes. You want the world to be better, fairer, prosperous, beautiful, safe, and resilient. You want your communities to be happy, safe, and well. You want your environment to thrive and children to grow old safely – and you want to pursue it all at once.

It's a tall order and a long bet. You'll try to shift the needle on issues requiring the cooperation and action of many people across many sectors, industries, groups, and stakeholders, most of whom don't agree. You'll make decisions now and won't know the outcomes for years or decades.

It won't be easy, but the stakes are high enough to try, and the shifts outlined in this book will help.

Strategic roles

Good, robust evidence shows that thinking, acting, and planning more strategically increases the likelihood of producing good outcomes.[9] But what does that look like?

Each of the three levels of the strategy landscape has its roles and responsibilities. Strategic leadership is when everyone does their job well – and nobody else's.

---

9   Vandersmissen et al., 2024.

The 'who' of strategy

WHO

Elected members
supported by
executive leaders

Executive leaders
supported by managers

Managers
supported by all staff

WHY
Values
Long-term direction
Community vision and outcomes

HOW
Systems and relationships
Organisational design
Strategic objectives

WHAT
Work plans
Projects
Budgets

Let's examine the 'who' for each level of the Strategy 101 model.

Elected members' role (the why)

In strategic Councils, 'why' activities are led by elected members and supported by executive leaders. Councillors formulate a shared vision and long-term direction for the community in a robust and transparent process facilitated and enabled by the executive leadership team. At the 'why' level, Councillors consider options, make decisions, and build relationships focused on long-term aspirational goals. They bring this outlook and perspective into all conversations and settings where they represent the Council.

Executive leaders' role (the how)

'How' activities are led by executive leaders, endorsed by elected members, and supported and implemented by managers. They work up; they work down.

Executive leaders present elected members with strategic options to pursue their long-term goals in the medium term, with transparency regarding each option's risks, costs, benefits, and potential payoffs. This helps elected members to make informed choices about medium-term priorities. Executive leaders then embed these priorities into organisational systems and communicate them clearly to managers. Managers use that guidance to prepare budgets, business plans, work programmes, and job descriptions. Executive leaders focus on reducing friction and making connections: they clarify focus, remove barriers, and design enabling systems and processes to support the why and how.

Managers' role (the what)

'What' level activities are led by Council managers, who take strategic direction and run with it, making operational choices about which projects to fund, which relationships to prioritise, what skills to develop, which people to hire, what funding to apply for, and which competing demand to put first. When they encounter challenges and barriers, they apply strategic priorities from the 'how' as a lens to shape their approach and adapt as they go. Managers communicate opportunities to improve the system to executive leaders. The results they deliver are daily proof of the Council's 'why'.

Aligning the roles

In strategic Councils, all three levels are aligned, with everyone playing their part. None is more important than the other, but each level requires different jobs and focus. If there is overcrowding at the bottom and a gaping hole in the middle, a directionless void is left at the top. This leaves Council staff trying to make decisions and deliver projects without direction – wasting time and money, diluting impact, and holding back progress.

The public value promise

If your Council looks more like the inverted triangle than the pyramid, your governance group and administration can do good things. You'll build shared understanding and meaning in your Council and community, strengthen relationships inside and outside Council, generate a more positive public image, and improve leadership coordination.[10] These changes mean you're more likely to have a productive organisation delivering quality services your citizens are satisfied with.[11]

Strategic Councils make better decisions, deliver better policy outcomes, and drive better organisational performance. They have a more trusting and engaged community, are more innovative and adaptive to change, and become more resilient and sustainable against external shocks. Operating at their highest potential, they can make meaningful local progress on globally critical issues such as social justice and climate change.

This is a prize worth having and one this book aims to steer you toward.

Chapter 1 summary

▪ Strategic local government leadership can leave a powerful legacy for generations to come.

▪ Councils provide critical community infrastructure beyond roads, rates, and rubbish.

▪ Strategy is critical for leaders who have limited resources and important goals.

---

10 George & Desmidt, 2014.
11 Poister et al., 2010.

- Strategy consists of three main components:
  - The 'why' level concerns long-term, aspirational direction.
  - The 'how' level includes medium-term, intentional design.
  - The 'what' level comprises short-term, operational delivery.
- Strategic Councils have a broad 'why', focused 'how', and clear 'what'.
- There are important differences between strategies in the private sector and public sector.
- Local government leaders with strategic skills lead productive organisations and deliver quality services to their communities.

02

From lagging to legendary

*'What you do makes a difference, and you have to decide
what kind of difference you want to make.'*

Jane Goodall

Councils are not like businesses; their aspirations, strategies, and deliverables differ. However, Councils are also sometimes confused with utility companies – especially in New Zealand and Australia, where local government has a uniquely constrained role due to the shape of our colonial history.[12]

Democracy would be an astonishingly inefficient way to run a utility company. Imagine it! 'We've established a company to maintain the roads, look after the pipes, and coordinate rubbish delivery. We'll invite people off the street to oversee the long-term plan, decisions, and budget – and check with everyone who lives here before we do anything major. It'll be fast and save money.'

---

12 Cookson, J., 2019.

Because businesses exist to capture private value in the form of profit, efficiency is king. Through direct transactions with consumers, businesses manage operations quickly and cheaply to capture the most private value possible and return it to shareholders. In business, autocracy makes sense.

When I ask Councillors why we have local government, they always tell me it's because local needs wouldn't be catered for without Councils. This is why Councils exist – to create public value for local communities. Councils collaborate with stakeholders to make decisions that improve outcomes across a diverse collective, upholding core community expectations such as integrity, transparency, engagement, and quality. In Councils, democracy is the most suitable option.

Democracy is a framework for fairness and representation, not speed.

Democracy is inefficient by design. It is a framework for fairness and representation, not speed. Democracy puts effectiveness before efficiency, and local democracy brings that to a community level, enabling local people to make choices that suit local needs.

Unlike the direct transactions of the private sector, it's not just people using Council services who benefit from them – the whole community does, whether they choose to or not. The value of public goods and services is harder to measure than in the private sector, as customer satisfaction is only one factor.

Creating public value means providing services that are infeasible or inequitable to deliver privately, such as roads, footpaths, and safety lighting. It includes providing services with collective benefit and individual disbenefit, such as fines and regulatory enforcement. These services often protect a shared, higher-order value like safety or justice. As Bligh Grant (2021) notes, 'The citizen who is a career criminal hardly benefits from a good criminal justice system, yet clearly the latter is a public good.'

Sometimes, local government intervenes in or compromises the private market. Public libraries aren't commercially viable and may compete with bookstores – but the value of universal literacy and accessible knowledge is an agreed social good. Wealthy citizens can build their own swimming pools or join an elite health club, but the community collectively endorses accessible and affordable swimming facilities, so the Council provides public pools.

Other times, the Council supports the private market. Large, multi-purpose infrastructure like roads, street lighting, water treatment, or community events centres are prohibitively expensive for a single company or industry to provide and run but attract many other industries and generate economic activity.

What public value looks like in local government

Creating public value is more complex than generating profit. It is driven by different factors, harder to measure in the short term, and more ambiguous to define. When in doubt, here are four factors to determine whether you're creating public value:

1. *Public value is a collective good.* Everyone in the community benefits, and it is difficult to exclude individuals from that benefit.

2. *Public value involves leveraged impact.* The provision of a service or protection of a value is a force multiplier that enables others.

3. *Public value has a sustained effect.* There is an observable and lasting shift in society or the community. This shift might be a service outcome, physical change, or intangible value shift, but it should stick around.

4. *Public value protects public values.* Investing in or backing this service, outcome, or idea contributes to or represents the

community's shared values and is usually a 'higher order' value (such as safety, justice, or health).

Here are a few examples of Council services that provide clear-cut public value:

- A public road is difficult to exclude people from using, facilitates economic and community activity, lasts for decades, and protects shared values: connection and mobility.

- A community event is a collective, non-excludable opportunity for people to unite. It protects shared values – belonging, unity, inclusion – and has leveraged effects beyond the event's timeframe.

Other examples require more debate and careful consideration. For example:

- Recreation facilities might be technically accessible but functionally inequitable, privileging some sporting codes over others or providing better facilities in wealthier parts of town. Do they still create public value?

- Pride Week or Indigenous language programmes redress discrimination but are seen by some community members to promote social division. Does the Council's support for these initiatives create public value?

These are not easy questions, nor do they have easy answers. Often, local government leaders make difficult decisions with conflicting values or sacrifice one value to promote another. These difficulties are why communities need elected representatives to consider such things.

We live in a time-poor, information-dense world with little time for reflection and introspection. Even if we are community-minded, most of us will not have time to consider how best to deliver public value; remembering to take out the bins after a busy day is hard enough. This is why we collectively delegate the responsibility for making these decisions.

Councils create local, long-term value that goes beyond the boundaries of the now, the urgent, and the commercial. They protect and pursue something important that the private market or higher tiers of government cannot.

> Councils create local, long-term value that goes beyond the boundaries of the now, the urgent, and the commercial.

Why we should use public value as the measure of success

We use many measures to determine whether Councils are effective and performing satisfactorily. Most of these are discrete time-bound KPIs tracking project delivery and community satisfaction. These are great for tracking operational progress but only tell part of the story.

A public value lens pushes the frame further out. Public value isn't about measuring adherence to an annual plan or even the delivery of a four-year plan. It is about the long-term value created for as many people as possible with lasting, positive outcomes. With public value as evaluation criteria, the more value you drive for the community, the better you do your job.

STRATEGIC CAPABILITY LEVELS

Let's look at the different levels of value created by Councils at different levels of strategic capability, from lagging to legendary.

The LOCAL Councils Model

Strategic capability	Key challenge	Development area	Public value
Legendary	Fear	Risk	100X
Ambitious	Focus	Decisions	10X
Compliant	Speed	Relationships	5X
Overwhelmed	Volume	Perspective	2X
Lagging	Dysfunction	Trust	1X

Lagging Councils

Lagging Councils are often dysfunctional. Politicians and officers pursue separate goals and agendas, leading to widespread frustration. People disagree about who should do what, and governance and organisational processes and policies are applied inconsistently. Councillors are mistrusting and suspicious, and Council managers are defensive and condescending. Stories about Council incompetence and dysfunction are in the news and on social media.

The prescription for overcoming dysfunction in a Lagging Council is to build trust, particularly within and between Councillors and staff.

Overwhelmed Councils

Overwhelmed Councils are busy and reactive, just keeping their heads above water. They spend lots of time answering emails, attending meetings, and dealing with emergencies. Staff feel 'overwhelmed but underutilised'.[13] The community is at its wits' end with the state of local infrastructure – though it tends to be the same

---

13   McKeown, G., 2014.

people complaining. Councillors don't understand why the Council can't get the basics right and often take on the mantle of constituent frustration.

The prescription for an Overwhelmed Council to manage volume is a more diverse and longer-term perspective.

Compliant Councils

Compliant Councils are keen to make things happen. This is often a 'Council of change', with a mandate to operate differently – perhaps after a failed project or a period of administration. Trust is low but rising, and people want to get things right. The signs are bright, but miscommunication and frustration still occur between Councillors and managers. There are too many papers to read, meetings run too long, and decisions get stuck.

The prescription for a Compliant Council to pick up the pace is to collaborate more productively.

Ambitious Councils

Ambitious Councils have big dreams and a long wish list, and they're making great progress. Councillors work together respectfully, use meeting time well, and stay (mostly) out of the weeds. There is a trusting relationship between the Council and the executive, but managers still tend to over-inform. Trust in policy and process is high, and staff and politicians freely suggest ideas for improvement. However, staff engagement levels can plateau, and burnout is a risk.

The prescription for an Ambitious Council to find focus is to make more strategic decisions.

Legendary Councils

Legendary Councils have a shared vision and alignment on priorities. Unnecessary bureaucracy is stripped away, and project delivery rates soar. There is high trust and demonstrable collegiality between elected members and executive managers. Councillors disagree without personal conflict and regularly reach a consensus. Executive managers give free and frank advice without fear or defensiveness. Decisions, once made, are accepted and not relitigated. The Council's community reputation is solid, and councillors help maintain an active and positive relationship with the media and stakeholders.

The prescription for a Legendary Council to move beyond fear is to take strategic risks.

***

You can assess your Council by filling out the strategic audit in the appendix.

Tips for improving your strategic capability

Local government faces three common strategic problems. Addressing these problems is the most effective way to transform your Council from lagging to legendary.

Problem 1
Short-termism weakens the Council's big-picture impact

Local government leaders are focused on short-term problems and lose sight of the bigger picture. This leads to wasted time and effort and unintended long-term consequences.

Addressing this requires *Shift 1: Perspective.*

Lift your gaze and leverage your impact. Expand your perspective to consider the horizon, significance, and context of your choices, and leave a legacy you can be proud of.

Problem 2
Misaligned objectives slow down the Council's progress

Councillors and Council managers are driven by different goals and outcomes. This disconnect leads to dysfunction and distrust.

Addressing this requires *Shift 2: Relationships*.

Do your job – and *only* your job. Unite leaders around a shared purpose and build governance and management relationships based on role clarity, reliance, and respect.

Problem 3
Unrealistic expectations dilute the Council's effectiveness

Councils with overambitious priorities cannot deliver. Scattered and inconsistent decisions dilute results, damage employee well-being, and spoil the Council's reputation.

Addressing this requires *Shift 3: Decisions*.

Create robust strategic decision processes. With clear direction, Council officers, stakeholders, and the community are empowered to do amazing things.

***

The following pages address these problems in turn, looking at the three shifts Councils can make to become more strategic and effective.

You will note these shifts align neatly with the first four 'development areas' in the LOCAL ladder. This book does not explicitly cover risk as a development area, though your appetite for strategic risk will improve and align as a result of expanding your perspective, enriching your relationships and enhancing your decisions.

Chapter 2 summary

- Local government creates local public value, which is more complex than generating profit. You can determine if you are creating public value using four criteria:
    - Public value is a collective good.
    - Public value involves leveraged impact.
    - Public value has a sustained effect.
    - Public value protects public values.
- Democracy is a framework for fairness and representation, not speed.
- Strategic local leadership creates more public value for more people over a longer time horizon.
- Councils operate at different levels of strategic capability, from lagging to legendary. Each level has its own distinct challenges.
- Councils face three common strategic problems: short-termism, misaligned objectives, and unrealistic expectations.

Why Glen Eira City Council expanded their perspective on community challenges

Every Council feels the pressure to be reactive, but not every Council commits to doing something about it. In 2022, Glen Eira City Council in south-east Melbourne reached a tipping point and decided it was time to change.

Glen Eira City Council CEO Rebecca McKenzie explains, 'We had new challenges around our financial sustainability. We had to make big decisions about what we do and don't do, what we invest in, and where we spend our time. We needed to stop reacting to immediate issues and think about our priorities, and we needed frameworks to navigate that change.'

Propelled by the enthusiasm and commitment of a senior Councillor and Council manager, Glen Eira committed their governance and management team to shared strategic development. The results have been phenomenal.

Councillor Jim Magee has been a member of Glen Eira Council for 16 years and been Mayor three times. He's learned the value of a strategic lens for the many demands on elected members. 'Every day, Council pushes you out of your comfort zone. I'm still waiting for two days to be the same. You're so busy, and you're taking a beating from the moment you wake up.'

The shift to becoming more strategic can be a personal challenge, especially when that causes tension in the local community.

McKenzie says, 'You can't please all the people all the time. So, there will be winners and losers. That's sometimes difficult.'

Working together to develop a bigger-picture perspective among Councillors and managers has had a marked impact on the way Glen Eira City Council operates. Mayor Anne-Marie Cade says, 'Elected members need to think big picture. Councillors can get caught in the weeds because the community constantly calls us. But we have limited time and resources. We need to prioritise. Operational issues are for the Council administration to solve. Councillors need to direct those questions to them and keep thinking big picture.'

Councillor Magee recalls, 'We discussed the importance of elected members standing on the mountain overseeing what's happening. We're looking down at the valley, but we're not part of what's happening there because that's not our job.'

McKenzie agrees. 'One thing that's been helpful is getting the Councillors to reflect on where they're spending their time and energy. We still get stuck talking about operational issues occasionally, but somebody will say, "Hang on a minute, are we in the paddock or are we on the peak?" That resets the level of the conversation.'

The benefits of a big-picture perspective are bigger than the changes it has made to individual Councillors. McKenzie says, 'The community are seeing greater consistency and integration in our strategies. And they benefit from seeing their elected Councillors working collaboratively towards a shared vision. Council's job is too difficult if you're dealing with internal strife.'

PERSPECTIVE

Expand your public value payoff
to leave a legacy.

03

From paddock to peak

In early 2020, I travelled to Vietnam to write my second book, *You Don't Need An MBA*.[14] It was a flawed trip. First, writing and sightseeing are not complementary activities. They're mutually exclusive – if you're doing one, you're not doing the other, so I always felt guilty.

Second, I hadn't considered the weather. Strategists are great for big-picture ideas but less useful for details like where to park the car, who will feed the cat – or what season it is in the country you're travelling to. The far north was cold and often wet.

On a writing break, my travelling companion and I visited a national park near Ninh Binh. We arrived in a fine mist of rain on a grey day. The lush green rice paddies I'd seen on Google were replaced by sludgy dirt littered with wisps of brown straw. Surveying the scrappy paddock, I grimaced. The prospect of walking up the famed 500-plus step walkway to Lying Dragon Mountain was now largely unappealing.

---

14   McKay, A., 2021.

Still, we'd come all this way, so up we went. The walk was tough, and we could only see a short distance before us, so we trudged up a seemingly endless stretch of steps, puffing and panting. Finally, we reached the top, and as I looked up, I gasped.

The view was spectacular.

Looking down across the valley, the sludgy paddocks transformed into an intricate, connected tapestry. Waterways weaved across the landscape, limestone crags jutted from the ground, and the fine mist trailed lazily across the fields. It was a magnificent vista, stretching as far as the eye could see. Suddenly, my annoyance at the weather and mud were embarrassingly trivial.

I noticed myself appreciating the seasons and how everything worked together. The peaceful fields recovering in the cool air, strewn with leftovers from the previous growing season, symbolise an essential and underappreciated time in the annual growing calendar. It's not as exciting as planting or harvesting, but the rest and recovery of winter are part of the cycle that enables the growth and fertility of spring.

What is the difference between the paddock and the peak? *Perspective.* In the paddock, I could only see the sludge in front of me, while at the peak, I appreciated the big picture.

PADDOCK PROBLEMS

Perspective matters, but it can only come from a distance. It's hard to appreciate the bigger picture when you're stuck in the paddock with muddy boots on.

When you're stuck in the paddock, you:

- Waste your limited time on matters that could have been resolved quickly or by somebody else.
- Get distracted from the most important points and leave critical issues undiscussed and decisions unmade.

- Develop a disproportionately negative view, focusing on problems rather than progress.
- Lose touch with the community's broader and diverse collection of views, beliefs, and experiences.
- Miss how choices in one area impact another – the consequences of a small gain might be a net loss, but you can't see it.
- Feel stuck and hopeless rather than aspirational and positive, which makes it less likely you will innovate or do exciting things.
- Make incorrect generalisations from one-off incidents because you haven't lifted your gaze far enough.

I call it the paddock and the peak. You might call it getting stuck in the weeds. Whatever you call it, it's easy to become trapped in the details. This is rarely due to ignorance or incompetence but usually because we're overwhelmed by information and too close to our problems.

Expanding perspective is a critical strategic shift for local government leaders who want to make high-quality decisions that benefit their community long term.

In this section

In this section, we will explore:

- The three most dangerous perspective traps.
- The three key elements of perspective.
- The importance of space.
- Practical interventions.

PERSPECTIVE TRAPS

Three dangerous traps prevent local government leaders from maintaining a useful perspective: the pragmatic trap, the present/urgent trap, and the public opinion trap.

The pragmatic trap

Local government rewards tangible action and attracts practical people. This can become a conflict when it's time for big-picture thinking and long-term decisions. The paddock is very attractive. It's where the action happens. When your job feels intangible, uncertain, or overwhelming, it's rewarding to tick things off a list and see progress – especially if you're a practical person seeking change.

The benefits of engaging in high-level conversations about intergenerational biodiversity outcomes, social equity, or municipality-wide spatial planning aren't always obvious. These conversations take months or years, few voters reward them, and the immediate outcomes can be disappointingly intangible. The future is uncertain, and these issues are unpopular, ignored, or have long payoff periods. So, why not redesign the rates notice, sort out the potholes, or focus on the footpaths instead?

The present/urgent trap

> 'Everything we hear is an opinion, not a fact.
> Everything we see is a perspective, not the truth.'
>
> Marcus Aurelius, *Meditations*

We're wired for the now, the close, and the urgent – the ringing phone, pinging email, or upcoming deadline. The things in front of us are tangible, present, and demanding, so we give them disproportionate attention.

In *Thinking, Fast and Slow*, Daniel Kahneman (2011) describes a collection of cognitive biases and heuristics related to this short-termism as 'What You See Is All There Is' (WYSIATI).

WYSIATI is a biological, evolutionary response to support survival – if a tiger in front of you wants to eat your face, contemplating the nature of life has little value. Instead, you activate a threat response and take immediate action. Our base instincts have maintained this vigilance in modern times, so we respond to the loudest, closest, most immediate phenomena (pinging notifications, emails, urgent reports) with the same survival instinct.

In local government, the operating environment and public pressure reinforce this bias for the short term. Election cycles and budget constraints pressure elected members to prioritise short-term achievements that are visible and tangible to voters. Long-term investments, with benefits which may not be realised for many years, are politically and financially challenging to justify – and are often punished in the polls.[15] People want the government to make their lives better *today*, future be damned.

The present/urgent trap is among the most dangerous traps local government leaders face. It is easy to become caught up in day-to-day tasks and forget the big picture. Leaders become overwhelmed by present demands and forget about long-term goals.

The public opinion trap

> '*Perhaps a man's character is like a tree, and his reputation like its shadow; the shadow is what we think of it; the tree is the real thing.*'
>
> Attributed to Abraham Lincoln

Have you called your electricity company recently, to say thanks? The conversation might go like this: 'I just wanted to say, on this sunny Friday afternoon, how much I appreciate your impact on my life this week. Thanks to your company, I've had continuous and reliable electricity that has improved every aspect of my personal and professional life. From hot water for showers and dishes to an internet connection for Zoom meetings, the power you've generated

---

15 Caplan, B., 2007.

for my household has been transformative. On my behalf, and hundreds of thousands of others: thank you.'

I bet you've never done this. You take electricity for granted and rarely think about it unless there's a brief interruption or a high bill to grumble about.

Local government leadership, done well, is like a utility. When it works, it's invisible. A marker of success is that the Council's reliable service provision and careful planning go largely unnoticed. Even when Councils go to great lengths to engage and share transparently with their community, the payoff can be disappointing.[16] People are busy, distracted, and uninterested.

> ## Local government leadership, done well, is like a utility.

But when services fail, or the Council does something they don't agree with – you'll soon know about it! When people say the Council doesn't listen to the community, they often mean Council didn't decide in their favour.

Public opinion is a terrible metric of success. First, research shows it is a poor predictor of public value creation.[17] Second, you probably don't know what it is. Public opinion is fluid, socially constructed, and difficult to pin down.[18] You're disproportionately likely to hear negative views, from a limited range of voices.

---

16 Sometimes, sharing more information actually decreases public perceptions of competence. In one study, which investigated the impact of making Council minutes available online, researchers found people who read the minutes were disappointed at the reality and chaos of public decision-making and formed negative views of the Council's competence (Grimmelikhuijsen, 2010). Indeed, transparency is often found to have a 'subdued and sometimes negative effect on trust in government'. (Grimmelikhuijsen et al., 2013).

17 Moore, 1995.

18 The very act of polling or surveying public opinion changes what public opinion is! (Herbst, 1998).

When local government leaders form their perspective from a limited, negative selection of voices, they lose perspective. They overlook things going well, form blind spots on issues with no public profile, and give excessive consideration to a few politically active constituents.

When you're doing a great job as a leader, you won't receive the praise you want from the people you want it from. Whether it's parenting ('Thanks for the curfew, it's kept me out of trouble.') or governance ('Due to your foresight, my grandchildren will live a better life.'), your best decisions may be unappreciated and unpopular.

Avoid trying to please a small portion of the community. Be wary of mistaking a vocal minority for a disgruntled majority or caring too much about 'reputation' and confusing it with character and integrity. Attempting to cater to public opinion can be a dangerous perspective trap.

PERSPECTIVE EXPANSION

There is an inherent perspective tension in the public sector. Marrying a long-term focus with regular elections, annual budgets, and quarterly performance reporting is challenging.[19] Overcoming this tension isn't easy, but it is transformative.

For communities to thrive long-term, we need local government leaders to shift their focus from short-term goals to long-term impacts and build tolerance for the frustration, sacrifice, and patience required for less tangible progress. This will open the door to sustainable and positive change for present and future generations.

When we expand our perspective, our potential impact enlarges. We consider bigger payoffs and longer timeframes to help more people and create lasting change. In the Eiffel Tower example, local

---

19 Höglund et al., 2018.

government leaders rose above the present/urgent complaints and wobbly public opinion.

They asked bigger, better questions about how to celebrate the unique character of Paris, honour the historical significance of the World Fair, and leave a mark on the future.

It's easy to spend your day bouncing from short-term fix to short-term fix. You'll always be busy, and you will achieve things that are worth celebrating. This is a perfectly reasonable way to lead. But it's not going to get you an Eiffel Tower.

When you expand your perspective, you:

- Spend most of your finite time, energy, and attention on matters that can only be resolved by Councillors and executive leaders.
- Put the most important issues and decisions first.
- Develop a balanced and holistic view of your community's needs.
- Become progress-oriented and focused on promising opportunities.
- Become aware of and understand multiple points of view.
- Attune to and empathise with your community's broad and diverse views, beliefs, and experiences.
- See how choices in one area might impact choices in another and strive to create a net gain across people, time, and space.
- Refuse to sacrifice long-term community well-being for short-term gain.
- Feel positive and hopeful about your community's future.
- Build coalitions of progress.
- Innovate, and do exciting things.
- Understand the trends and shifts in your community to avoid making incorrect generalisations from one-off incidents.

These skills come more naturally to some than others, but they can be learned and embedded into working practices.

The three elements of perspective

Expanding your perspective requires you to consider three things:

- **Horizon:** *time* and *distance.*
- **Significance:** *relative impact* and *potential permanence.*
- **Context:** *patterns* and *connections.*

Chapter 3 summary

- Being stuck in the details (the paddock) prevents seeing the bigger picture (the peak).

- Local government leaders face three dangerous perspective traps: the pragmatic trap, the present/urgent trap, and the public opinion trap, which hinder long-term strategic thinking.

- Local government leaders should expand their perspective to focus on long-term impacts, build tolerance for frustration and patience, and make decisions that benefit the community in the long run.

- The three elements of strategic perspective are horizon (time and distance), significance (relative impact and permanence), and context (patterns and relationships).

04

Horizon

'The health of the eye seems to demand a horizon.
We are never tired, so long as we can see far enough.'

Ralph Waldo Emerson

In *80/20 Sales and Marketing*, Perry Marshall (2013) proposes a time management framework for salespeople and entrepreneurs. He believes people spend too much time on trivial $10-per-hour tasks like running errands and basic administration and too little time on $1000- or $10,000-per-hour tasks like building client relationships or public speaking.

The dollar figures aren't relevant to local government because we don't capture financial value; we create public value. Efficiency is not our primary aim. However, the theory stands up when we replace the dollar figures with *decision payoff periods*.

Three elements of perspective

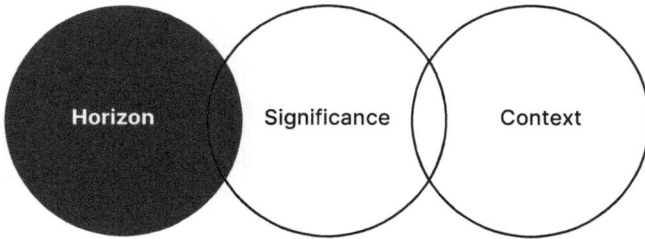

PERSPECTIVE PAYS OFF

Think of Council as making decisions with varying payoff periods (the length and magnitude of benefits provided), ranging from 10 minutes to 10 decades. For example, resolving a service request might result in a 10-minute payoff when the community member who complained is satisfied. Supporting local businesses through tight financial times like a recession might have a 10-month payoff. New community facilities might have a 10-year payoff, while investing in urban shade might have a 10-decade payoff.

When local government leaders waste time on inconsequential issues, it can exponentially impact your community's future. When you use limited time, attention, and conversation for minor issues, you forgo space for more important concerns. These choices compound over time, yet the time it takes to make those decisions may vary little. It can take just as long to make a 10-minute decision as a 10-year decision.

When local government leaders are strategic in their outlook, they drive long-term public value for people in their communities. This can be understood as a public value payoff.

Public value payoff

Strategic level	Outcome	Public value payoff
WHY	Legacy	1:10,000+
HOW	Progress	1:100–1:1000
WHAT	Performance	1:1–1:10

Consider these examples:

- Responding to an individual service request (a 'what' job) will benefit one person, family, or street. The public value payoff at this level would be between 1:1 and 1:10, and many people are employed to deliver this outcome.

- Building a stakeholder relationship, designing an organisational process, or reviewing a key policy ('how' jobs) will affect many more people over a longer period. The public value payoff at this level is between 1:100 and 1:1000. Depending on the size of your Council, 10 to 50 people do this work.

- Adopting an infrastructure or urban planning strategy, building social housing, striking a City Deal with the government, or committing resources to climate mitigation ('why' jobs) are at another level entirely. Over multiple generations, these decisions may affect hundreds of thousands of people. The public value payoff at this level starts at 1:10,000, and only a dozen people in your organisation can deliver these outcomes. The impact at this level is highly leveraged, though significantly less tangible, and more challenging to quantify in the short term.

When local government leaders focus on decisions that only they are able to make, and push out the decision horizon, they maximise their public value payoff.

Broadening our horizon and increasing our potential payoff period means considering *time* and *distance*. Either component might change our thoughts about certain decisions.

TIME HORIZONS

> *'There is an absence of institutional mechanisms that give voice to the interests of tomorrow's generations, who are effectively disenfranchised from the system. Politics enables the colonisation of the future.'*
>
> Krznaric, 2020

Politics scales individual choices and ideas for greater collective impact. While local politics is constrained by geography and other tiers of government, pushing out the time horizon can change the trajectory of a community's future.

Time is about more than numbers. The Ancient Greeks had two words for time: chronos and kairos. *Chronos* is quantitative time – watches, calendars, times, and dates. *Kairos*, which roughly translates to 'the right time', is qualitative timeliness – occasions with profound significance.

We can apply both concepts to the Eiffel Tower example. While counting down to the Exposition Universelle was in *chronos*, acting boldly to mark France's position on the world stage was about *kairos* – the opportunity to create a moment of historical significance.

Strategic leaders aiming for legacy consider both *chronos* and *kairos*, time and timeliness.

In *The Good Ancestor*, Roman Krznaric (2020) claims we have two 'brains' – a 'marshmallow brain' fixated on short-term desires and rewards and an 'acorn brain', which enables us to plant seeds, think long-term and work toward bigger goals. The acorn brain is an evolutionary advantage that's generated compounding rewards throughout history.

Krznaric argues that the design and short-term focus of our current political systems unfairly imposes on future generations the consequences of technological change and environmental degradation. Will Macaskill's seminal text *What We Owe the Future: A million-year view* sums it up beautifully thus: 'Future people count.'[20]

Considering the long-term is inescapable in local government. Infrastructure has a useful life of many decades, and decisions about planning and the environment shape your place for future generations. But whether this is done with perspective is another matter.

Considering the long-term is inescapable in local government.

By taking a long-term view, you can make meaningful progress toward more sustainable and resilient communities. For example, investments in green infrastructure and renewable energy won't add up in a three- to five-year Council or CEO term. But when we expand the investment payback period, recognise intergenerational benefits, and consider non-financial gains, the payoff is phenomenal. Mitigating long-term environmental impacts and reducing dependency on non-renewable resources could change the future shape of your community.

---

20 Macaskill, W., 2022.

Decisions about environmental, social, and community well-being don't pay off quickly or directly – and when they do, it's not Council who reaps the results. Leaving a legacy requires a longer-term view and enduring the interim flack and costs, which will never be easy in a short-term political environment hamstrung by a lack of funding and support.

DISTANCE HORIZONS

Attaining distance in a local community can be difficult – how can you be objective about something you care about, affecting people you know, in a place you're connected to?

You can't – and you shouldn't. Your local connection and knowledge qualify you for this job, and the community values your investment. But be careful of confusing your passion for accuracy. Most decisions you make as a local government leader concern uncertain futures, emerging issues, conflicting beliefs, and ambiguous outcomes. Accuracy is unattainable.

Under these conditions, distance is about expanding your portfolio of perspectives to consider multiple points of view. The ability to inhabit a new perspective is a uniquely human gift. If we have the right access point, we can attune to the feelings of others, whether we have all the details or not. The more points of view you understand, the more nuance and empathy your decisions will have.

In workshops with Councils, I often ask them to role-play. We generate a long list of potential points of view around different categories, such as:

- Occupation (farmer, business owner, teacher, retail worker).
- Age (child, elderly, unborn).
- Location (urban, rural, out-of-state).
- Species (people, birds, fish, cows).

- Time (50 years ago, now, 100 years in the future).
- Customer (public transport user, consent applicant).
- Religion, culture, socioeconomic status, political affiliation … and so on.

Then, we try on different perspectives to consider different issues.

The wider and further we stretch our perspective, the more distance we attain from our gut reactions, instincts, and unconscious biases. The more conscious we are of how our personal points of view and lived experiences influence our position, the richer the conversation becomes and the less attached we become to being 'right'.

Perspective asks us to inhabit multiple points of view, and we can only do that if we attain personal distance. It asks us to consider questions like:

- How would you feel about your choices if you were far into the future, looking back?
- How would you feel about your choices if you were somebody else?

Once you give up on the idea that there's a correct way to think about an issue, you lean into complexity and grapple with the difficulty. You can inhabit and experiment with a full suite of different – sometimes conflicting – beliefs, values, and experiences.

Perspective isn't just about getting out of the weeds. Your role as a local government leader is also to connect and relate to the experience of the people who live in your community. Distance isn't about disconnection; distance creates space for diversity and empathy. When you know what others are going through – not just the perspectives you're closest to – and truly understand the impact on their lives, you can bring that empathy into your decisions for everyone's benefit.

Chapter 4 summary

▪ Expanding your horizon increases the payoff periods of your decisions.

▪ 'Horizon' consists of both *time* and *distance*.

▪ Time can be quantitative *(chronos)* or qualitative *(kairos)*.

▪ Long-term thinking leverages your potential impact.

▪ Distance is not about disconnection; it's about diversity.

▪ Diversity of perspective enables empathy.

05

Significance

*'You can not overestimate the unimportance of
practically everything.'*

John Maxwell

I vividly remember my first 10-year plan process – I was excited to
see behind the scenes of such important decisions!

By day three of budget workshops, my excitement was long gone.
Councillors and managers sat with A3 landscape books before
them – hundreds of pages of tiny, printed budgets. Line by line, we
went through the projections for every Council department and
activity, with Councillors raising questions as we went. Yawn.

This was a big year for budget decisions. This Council had one of the
largest unsealed road networks in the country. It had been locked
in negotiations with the government for years about increasing the
level of funding assistance. After years of frustration, the Council
made a big call and decided to fund millions in unsubsidised road
maintenance. It was a big decision that was made surprisingly
quickly, with the vote passing in just a few minutes.

Some time later, going through the corporate services budget, a Councillor pushed their microphone button to query a line in the budget.

'What's this $15,000 for catering?'

The Chief Financial Officer looked up casually and uttered a phrase he would come to regret. 'Oh, that? It's the cheese budget.'

Cue: furore.

The budget was for supplies provided to the Council's in-house morning tea lady. Every morning, at 10 am, Council staff were treated to tea, coffee, and cheese on crackers. Every afternoon, at 3 pm, tea, coffee, and biscuits – on Friday: Tim Tams. On days that Councillors attended meetings or workshops, they enjoyed the same treatment.

Every elected member had something to say about this. Accusations of irresponsible public spending flew across the room. More than one Councillor valiantly offered to bring packed lunches to Council meetings. After 45 minutes of discussion and debate, it was finally resolved. Firstly, our morning tea lady had worked for Council for almost 30 years. She was a pillar of the local community, and nobody was willing to cross her. Secondly, everyone liked the cheese. The cheese budget stayed.

Four minutes of discussion for an extra $2 million in unsealed road improvements; 45 minutes for the $15,000 cheese budget. The first decision carried significant consequences for the overall rates increase and Council's debt cap. The second decision didn't dent the budget but came with fears of public pushback. The payoff period of the first decision: years. The payoff period for the second: minutes.

I've told that story at many different Councils and it always elicits knowing and embarrassed laughter, as people nudge each other with their elbows and talk about their equivalent of the 'cheese budget'.

Three elements of perspective

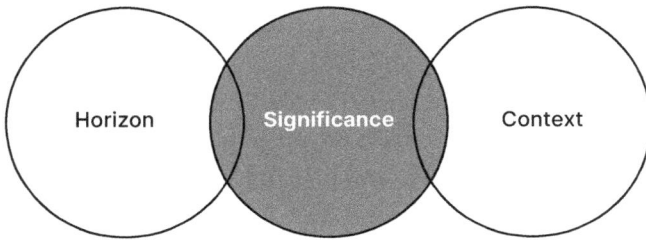

SIGNIFICANCE DIMENSIONS

Not all problems are created equally, but it can be difficult to tell when they're in front of us. The direct community connection that makes Council so valuable is the double-edged sword that drags local government leaders into the minutiae.

In a corporate environment or at other levels of government, leaders aren't told about barking dogs or potholes, and there are layers of separation between decision-maker and end user. In local government, that separation doesn't exist.

To compound that, local government leaders are, without exception, people who care deeply about their place and the people in it. When you're a person who cares, and someone tells you about a problem, it's tough not to get sucked in.

But problems are like cockroaches and glitter: persistent. The number of potential problems to solve is infinite, so local government leaders should make decisions based on significance, which includes two dimensions: *relative impact* and *potential permanence.*

Problems are like cockroaches and glitter: persistent.

RELATIVE IMPACT

People are poor intuitive assessors of risk. We underestimate the likelihood of common issues like temporary disability and overestimate the likelihood of rare and serious crime.[21] We insure our homes but not our incomes. We are bullish on our ability to predict an unlikely future and blind to the changes happening right before us.

For these reasons, people are poorly equipped to make instinctive assessments about the significance of a decision. When I run strategic risk workshops with Councils, we throw out the traffic lights and likelihood matrices because the biggest risks aren't predictable. By concentrating on *impact* rather than likelihood, we focus on things with the biggest potential effect on our goals.

Impact puts things into perspective, asking: how big a deal is this to us, our community, and the pursuit of our goals? When deciding the relative impact of an issue, question, or opportunity, consider the full range of costs and effects that may result from action or lack of action, including social, cultural, financial, and environmental costs, now and in the future.

Questions to put impact into perspective:

▪ What is the potential impact of this problem?

▪ To how many people?

▪ Who will be affected the most?

▪ What effect will this have on the achievement of our goals?

▪ What is the cost of this – financially, socially, and otherwise – now and into the future?

But considering impact is not enough – something can be important without being the *most* important. Local government leaders must

---

21 Kahneman, D., 2011.

focus on only the most important things because otherwise you'll run out of time and attention before you get to them.

To consider relative impact, ask:

- How does this compare to other decisions we're facing?
- Are we allocating our attention correctly?
- Should we move on or delegate this?

POTENTIAL PERMANENCE

Did you keep a diary as a teenager? High emotions poured onto the page, only to be forgotten. On a re-read, those impassioned entries make us cringe.

While we're no longer teenagers, we're still prone to misjudge how permanent a crisis or feeling will be. Some things feel very big and important today but are easily forgotten in the scheme of things. Look at your calendar from a year ago and review what you were focused on – how many are as big as they felt at the time? How many had you completely forgotten?

In Council, small dramas and cheese budgets *feel* huge. We're stuck in the paddock, looking at what's in front of us, and it's looming large. Once we climb the peak, we remember winter is only a season, and the sun will come out again. If we make choices based on winter conditions, we'll feel stupid when spring comes.

Some decisions, problems, issues, or opportunities are permanent but largely inconsequential. In those cases, we should be careful not to analyse them to death or try to perfect our approach. Those choices can often be delegated. Others are consequential, but temporary. In those cases, we should make the best decision for the short term and await changes or feedback to review and adapt.

The most important issues have more permanent consequences or long-term significance but these are often less urgent. Winter will give way to spring every year – but climate change might shorten, prolong, or intensify the different seasons, increase the chance of catastrophic crop loss through natural disasters, and affect the yearly harvest for decades. These issues need a different level of care. An irreversible decision has greater significance than a reversible one.

Questions to put permanence into perspective:

- How long will this be an issue for?
- Will we remember this in the future?
- How permanent are the consequences of this decision?
- Will we be able to change direction once we've made this choice?

Chapter 5 summary

- Establishing significance leads to better use of limited time.

- There are unlimited problems to solve.

- Assess significance by considering relative impact and potential permanence.

- Relative impact considers consequences.

- Potential permanence distinguishes between reversible and irreversible choices.

06

Context

'Learn how to see. Recognise that everything
connects to everything else.'

Leonardo da Vinci

On the peak in Vietnam, looking across the valley, I appreciated winter's kairos, or timeliness. Once I got over my disappointment, I realised that while the rest and recovery of winter are not as exciting as the growth and fertility of spring, it's part of the cycle that makes fertility possible.

It also became easier to appreciate the connection between things – the fields, the waterways meandering between them, the weather, the seasons, and the impact of people like me trekking uphill for the perfect Instagram shot and disrupting the balance of the environment.

In a complex system like the environment, a change in one part affects the others. Well-meaning interventions have unexpected consequences.

When grey wolves were driven to extinction in the early 21st century in Yellowstone National Park, a 'trophic cascade' occurred and elk populations boomed out of control. Without enough food, the herds became unhealthy and began to starve. Once the grey wolves, predators to elk, were reintroduced in 1995, elk herds became healthier and more resilient. Removing the predator had disrupted the health of the whole system. Interestingly, the return of the wolves hasn't just been good for the elk. Trees have benefited too. With the elk population under control and grazing differently due to the presence of wolves, the trees thrive, too.[22] In a complex system, everything is connected, and it's not always obvious how – especially when you can only see one part at a time.

Three elements of perspective

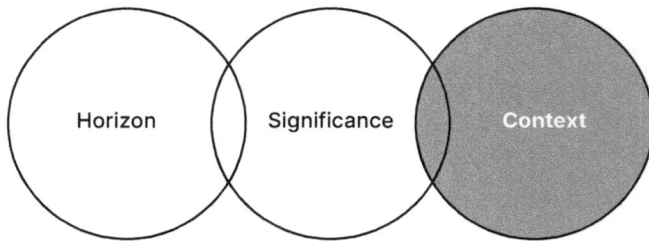

COMMUNITY SYSTEMS

Communities are complex systems. A diverse group of actors interacts at different levels across a fabric of social and cultural variation. Many externalities – regulatory, environmental, technological, social, cultural, and economic – affect the system, making it difficult to attribute specific inputs to certain outputs. Councils are just one actor and have little direct control over the environment in which they operate.

---

22 Ripple, W. J., Larsen, E. J., Renkin, R. A., & Smith, D. W., 2001.

Systems thinking is a core skill for a local government leader. Just as you influence your environment, your environment influences how you think and make decisions and will affect the outcomes and implementation of those decisions.[23] You've never been in a room you weren't in. Without the skills to appreciate and recognise context, you risk intervening in one area and worsening broader outcomes.

Joining the dots requires moving beyond the details of an individual situation, example, or problem to consider *patterns* and *connections*.

PATTERNS

The plural of anecdote is not evidence. The plural of pothole is not pattern.

Local government leaders are connected to their communities. They often receive impassioned and frustrated constituents' thoughts on the state and quality of the local infrastructure and service delivery.

> ## The plural of anecdote is not evidence.
> ## The plural of pothole is not pattern.

To make things worse, people are hardwired for negativity – we pay more attention to bad things than good, making them seem more prevalent than they are. When we only hear negative stories, it's easy to extrapolate individual examples to a catastrophic picture and fear the community is falling apart.

Pattern recognition helps local government leaders understand the full picture. When local government leaders focus on trends rather than individual events, they use their limited resources more effectively.

---

23   Vandersmissen & George, 2023.

If you're a Councillor and you've received 10 pothole complaints this month, you might assume that potholes are a big problem and things are worsening. But to examine the pattern, you would pause judgement or assumptions and ask questions like:

▪ Are there more potholes at this time of year than usual?

▪ Have pothole complaints been increasing or decreasing?

▪ How has community satisfaction changed overall? What else is affecting and being affected by these changes?

▪ Has our road maintenance been on schedule? Why or why not?

These questions look for patterns rather than particulars.

Questions to focus on patterns, not particulars:

▪ What is the trend? Are things getting worse or better?

▪ Has anything happened that has affected this?

▪ What broader category of 'things' is this issue part of? How is the overall category performing? Why?

▪ What are the causes of this problem? What are the consequences?

CONNECTIONS

'A system is not the sum of the behaviour of its parts;
it's a product of their interactions.'

Dr Russell Ackoff [24]

Communities are complex systems with close relationships and often unexpected causes and effects, yet the public sector is often poor at using systems approaches to policy challenges.

---

24   Brant, S., 2010, 1994.

Government agencies attempt to break problems into parts, hoping for efficiency. Separate departments specialise in energy, land, food, air, water, wildlife, economy, finance, and building regulations. These entities compete for limited budgets, leading to the pursuit of disconnected or even conflicting agendas.

Local government has an advantage: its close relationships and diverse services offer a more integrated community view. Councils understand that the quality of the relationship between environmental health inspectors and businesses might have as much impact on compliance levels as the regulations themselves. Councils see the impact of urban green belts and walkways on everything from biodiversity to active recreation rates and property values.

Systems thinking recognises a system is not the sum of its parts but the product of its interactions. Communities have collective properties – cohesion, safety, resilience, connection – that no one person has in isolation. These properties are generated by the relationships and connections within and between people and the environment.

> **Systems thinking recognises a system is not the sum of its parts but the product of its interactions.**

Each part of the system interacts with other parts of the system as a constraint, enabler, dependent, or partner. Things that don't make sense individually will sometimes make sense in context, and things that make sense individually won't always make sense in the big picture.

This effect is noticeable for Councils with ward-based elections. Councillors elected by a particular ward may pursue outcomes and projects for their ward that negatively affect the broader community or resist municipality-wide change, which would benefit the whole community but negatively affect their ward.

Implementing paid parking on the main street against the opinion of local shoppers might cause a few grumbles. Still, it makes sense when regular vehicle turnover increases foot traffic for local shops and makes the city more vibrant.

Systems thinkers understand the best way to improve a system's outcomes is not to view the parts separately but to consider how they connect. This helps us find creative solutions, solve tricky problems, and deliver important outcomes.

For example:

- Achieving better safety outcomes in the city might not require better streetlights but instead need closer timing alignment between city events and public transport.
- Supporting economic growth for local businesses might not be best achieved by providing grants but by marketing to tourists or investing in recreation facilities.

These questions look at the impact of relationships and connection points.

Questions to focus on connections:

- What and who else is this outcome dependent on? What influence do we have on that?
- What are our biggest constraints and barriers to progress? How can we shift our relationship to those things?
- What else might be affected by a change in this area? How?

Chapter 6 summary

- Communities are complex systems and require systems thinking.
- Context interrogates patterns and connections.
- Patterns are about trends and changes over time.
- Connections are about how different parts of the system interact.

07

Perspective in practice

In May 2015, a *Time* magazine headline captured global attention: 'You Now Have a Shorter Attention Span Than a Goldfish!'

The article's opening paragraph continued: 'The average attention span for the notoriously ill-focused goldfish is nine seconds, but according to a new study from Microsoft Corp., people now generally lose concentration after eight seconds, highlighting the effects of an increasingly digitalized lifestyle on the brain.'[25] Between 2000 and 2015, the average adult's attention span dropped from twelve seconds to eight seconds.

The 'goldfish effect' made news worldwide, but the true story is more complex. First, goldfish can remember things for up to five months.[26] Second, our attention span is not smaller; it's fuller. A 2019 University of Denmark study found our collective attention span is overtaxed.[27] The accelerating volume and speed of content exhaust attention more quickly than in the past. We're processing more

---

25 McSpadden, K., 2015.
26 SPCA.
27 Lorenz-Spreen, P., Mønsted, B. M., Hövel, P., & Lehmann, S., 2019.

information – ads, content, articles, group chats, emails, news – and that information constantly changes.

PERSPECTIVE THREATS

In a world awash with information, sensationalism, clickbait, disconnection, and division, there are two main threats to perspective: density and proximity. Overcoming these powerful forces requires space.

Density

When things become too dense, our perspective weakens. We focus on the details, try to solve each problem as it arises, and can't see how things fit together. This trap can also lead to analysis paralysis, where we spend so much time trying to understand the problem that we never act.

Density can be a problem in Council and committee reports. When information is too much, too technical, and too deep, a layman reader struggles to locate the salient facts or process their implications.

Proximity

> 'There is no such thing as the view from nowhere, or everywhere for that matter. Our point of view biases our observation, consciously and unconsciously. You cannot understand the view without the point of view.'
>
> Noam Shpancer, *The Good Psychologist*

The closer you are to a problem, the less perspective you have on its true importance. Proximity can be physical – as in, you're looking at it – or conceptual, such as subject matter expertise and echo chambers. Physical proximity is an easy fix, but conceptual proximity requires intention to overcome.

Expertise

Expertise is critical to understand how things work, identify what's possible and generate solutions. It can also lead to narrow thinking.

Our expertise can make it hard to challenge our assumptions, especially if we've been in a job or sector for a long time. We become vulnerable to Maslow's Law of the Instrument ('when all you have is a hammer … '), and we rely too much on familiar tools. As an engineer, you see engineering solutions. As a business owner, you view community issues through a business lens.

Echo chambers

Myopia is an environmental inevitability in a world that pushes us into echo chambers. Whether on social media, at work, or in community groups, we surround ourselves with people who think like we do, read the same things, and have similar experiences.

In an echo chamber, our opinions are reflected back to us, reinforcing our beliefs and biases. We start to think there's a 'right' answer or that we understand a situation better than others. It's comfortable, but it can also be dangerous, leading to groupthink and a failure to consider alternative perspectives.

***

Together, density and proximity constrain our capacity for perspective.

PERSPECTIVE ENABLERS

*'We must have some room to breathe. We need freedom
to think and permission to heal. Our relationships
are being starved to death by velocity.
No one has the time to listen, let alone love.'*

Richard A. Swenson

The *Time* article was wrong about goldfish, but some of its advice on overcoming attention deficits is useful. Readers are advised not to email first thing in the morning or last thing at night, not to agree to meetings or calls without a clear agenda and end time, to schedule set times for batch processing emails, avoid letting people 'ramble' in conversations, and have smartphone-free time during the week.

These attention hacks all have one thing in common: their attempt to create some space. Perspective needs physical, mental, and temporal space.

Physical space

Have you ever walked from the living room to the kitchen to get something, only to reach the kitchen and forget what you went there for? This is the 'doorway effect' – our brain resets in different physical environments. The same is true in the other direction – we are programmed to think and feel a certain way in certain environments.

Be aware of your physical environment to create strategic space and channel a broader perspective. If Council meetings are in Chambers, hold workshops in a different room. Have stakeholder meetings on-site. Hold walking meetings. Host your strategy days in different venues.

Mental space

Information density crowds our capacity for contemplation. Engaging our internal sorting hat becomes difficult when we have too much information to process. Be mindful of your information diet – garbage in means garbage out. If your limited attention is devoted to social media trolls, constituent complaints, or clickbait news, your thoughts and perspective will reflect that.

Creating mental space requires intention about your attention. Be aware of the sources of your information and carve out moments in your day and week for contemplation.

Temporal space

Thinking takes time, and this time will not appear organically. Block out time for important thinking. Create a buffer around important tasks and meetings and leave a margin for unexpected issues.

When you can't create any additional time, use your existing time differently. Focus conversations on strategic items and delegate operational items to others. Remove unnecessary meetings, ignore irrelevant emails, and forward complaints to the correct department. Create time and space for speaking with people, building relationships, reading reports, and engaging with your colleagues. There is no elevator from the paddock to the peak.

> There is no elevator from the paddock to the peak.

PERSPECTIVE FLEXIBILITY

All this long-term thinking is useful and important – but when shit hits the fan, it might not be useful to gaze from the mountaintop.

Local government leaders need to stay flexible and responsive to deal with disasters, unexpected changes, or even – with any luck – opportunities.

Many of the things affecting local government are immediate and unexpected: natural disasters, economic downturns, public health emergencies, and community crises. The community will suffer unless local government leaders can respond immediately. Taking charge of your perspective doesn't constrain responsiveness; it improves the quality of your response. With a long-term lens, we make better short-term choices.

Strategic local government leaders zoom out when they miss the pattern and zoom in when they miss the point. Distance does not have to mean disconnection. We can remain responsive and connected by developing perspective flexibility.

Perspective flexibility helps adjust our lens. You'll know you're too close when you become unreasonably attached to a particular solution or outcome or when the problem feels too messy or unsolvable. You'll know you're too far away when the problem seems too simple or the people involved seem unreasonable.

Perspective allows us to be clearer about how we respond to unexpected change and do it more quickly, in alignment with our goals and values. But it is a spectrum. You will naturally lean further one way; the most effective leaders know when to lean back the other.

When you're too close, attain distance:

- Take a longer view.
- Compare to others.
- Check relative impact.
- Interrogate trends.
- Consider connections.

When you're too far away, attune with empathy:

▯ Put yourself in someone else's shoes.

▯ Take a shorter view.

▯ Ask for details.

▯ Consider exceptions.

PERSPECTIVE INTERVENTIONS

Here are some practical ways to expand perspective among Councillors and Council managers.

Embed perspective diversity into reports and decision processes

Perspective can form part of your decision processes. To operationalise perspective, ensure reports and document templates like business cases, funding requests, and Council reports incorporate horizon, significance, and context. Council recommendations should consider long-term impacts and outline potential consequences and effects for as many people as possible.

> **Templates for Council papers and business cases might include sections on:**
>
> ▯ Horizon: decision payoff periods and conflicting views.
>
> ▯ Significance: relative impact and potential permanence.
>
> ▯ Context: patterns and connections.

Seek diverse opinions and views

With a full range of views, opinions, and beliefs, it is easier to gain perspective on a situation, draw connections between different parts of the system, and see significance clearly.

To achieve perspective diversity:

- Invite new and different voices to the Council table.
- Build relationships with new people and stakeholders.
- Speak directly with affected parties, preferably on site.
- Role-play in workshops.
- Read widely to understand the debates on an issue.
- Appoint a 'devil's advocate' to interrogate prevailing logic.

Prioritise mental, temporal, and physical space

Space will not happen by accident. Finding the space to think more about your role and community will require intentional scheduling and agreement with your peers.

To prioritise space:

- Schedule governance-only and governance/executive offsites, away days, or strategy time, at least quarterly.
- Allocate strategy space in your calendar each week.
- Protect meeting and forum time by keeping a careful agenda, limiting operational conversations, and prioritising the most important items.

Ask bigger, better questions

When presented with new information, we default to asking small questions. This is not because we have small minds but because we're overwhelmed and trying to be useful. Specific, detail-focused questions will deliver specific, detail-focused responses. They trap us in a cycle of putting out short-term fires and limit our ability to make big-picture, long-term changes.

Instead, local government leaders can ask bigger, better questions.

Levels of questioning

Level 3	Evaluation	**WHY** does this matter?	Alignment Risk Impact
Level 2	Exploration	**HOW** does this work?	Trends Changes Trade-offs
Level 1	Explanation	**WHAT** happened?	Facts Figures Specifics

When leaders ask bigger, better questions, they waste less time, make more progress, and have more meaningful (and less frustrating) conversations. It's not always appropriate or useful to ask a level 3 question, but it is almost always useful to move to level 2.

Let's look at the different levels of questioning.

Level 1: Explanation

Most people get stuck here. They ask what's happened so far and what needs to happen next. They get trapped in the details, and time goes down the drain. These questions tend to provoke defensiveness, blame, over-explanation, and mistrust.

Level 1 questions:

- *What is happening with the footpath on Main Street?*
- *Why is that repair taking so long?*
- *Why hasn't my neighbour heard back from Council?*

Level 2: Exploration

Level two questions encourage a systems mindset. We look for trends, connections, and insights that relate to more than one problem.

These questions remove the focus from people, limit the potential for blame, and open discussion about barriers and enablers.

Level 2 questions:

- *How is our footpath renewals programme progressing?*
- *Has customer satisfaction changed over the last year?*
- *Are we meeting our response times for service requests?*

Level 3: Evaluation

Level three questions put problems and issues into broader perspective, evaluating their importance and potential impact by thinking wider, deeper, and longer-term. At this level of abstraction, we anchor back to our big-picture goals and direction and evaluate our options and choices with those in mind.

Level 3 questions:

- *Does the funding for our maintenance programme reflect our priorities?*
- *Do we have an infrastructure strategy for the long term?*
- *What are our service levels for urban areas? Are they still appropriate?*

***

Quality questions are bigger, broader, and more strategic. They look beyond people and problems, assume positive intent, and adopt compassionate curiosity to get to the bigger picture and effect real change.

When local government leaders ask better questions, they get better answers and the whole community benefits.

Chapter 7 summary

- Density and proximity hinder our ability to maintain perspective.

- Leaders must prioritise physical, mental, and temporal space.

- Use horizon, significance, and context in decisions and seek diverse opinions.

- Schedule strategy sessions, invite diverse voices, protect strategic time, and ask bigger, better questions.

Perspective in summary

- Perspective helps local government leaders make high-quality decisions that benefit their community long term.

- There are three main perspective traps: the present/urgent trap, the pragmatic trap, and the public opinion trap.

- Perspective requires a shift in thinking from the paddock to the peak.

- The three key elements of perspective are:
  - **Horizon:** to expand the length and breadth of our impact.
  - **Significance:** to focus attention and energy on things that matter.
  - **Context:** to appreciate relationships and create net community benefit.

- Proximity and density are the two biggest threats to perspective. Perspective needs physical, mental, and temporal space.

- Perspective flexibility requires attaining distance when we are too close to a situation and attuning with empathy when we are too detached.

- Practical ways to expand perspective include:
  - Operationalise horizon, significance, and context as part of decision processes.
  - Provide high-quality information that supports perspective, including trend analyses and data.
  - Create physical, mental, and temporal space through scheduled workshops and offsites.
  - Seek a more diverse array of perspectives.
  - Ask bigger, better questions.

How Mildura Rural City Council reset their relationships

In 2022, Mildura Rural City Council was regrouping after an extensive external review.

Mayor Liam Wood recalls, 'The review went through the whole organisation from head to toe, and there was a real air of change. I'd just become Mayor, so I wanted to do some training with the Councillors – focus inward, understand our dynamic, and how we can best represent our community. You do this kind of development in any other organisation, and it's just as important in local government.'

Mayor Wood explains how overwhelming Council can be at the start: 'There are so many rules, and you get thrown in the deep end. You're expected to put the gloves on and become a surgeon overnight.' Council CEO Martin Hawson agrees, 'Councillors get elected, and suddenly they're responsible for an organisation with a $200 million budget. They're expected to become remarkable strategic leaders overnight, when they may not yet even understand the full parameters of their role.'

Hawson is under no illusions about the difficulty his elected counterparts face: 'It's challenging for Councillors to stay out of the operational weeds because they're acting on behalf of the community. It's hard to stay in the strategic zone when you get calls at nine at night saying the footpath has a crack!'

Role clarity, Hawson believes, is the ticket to finding balance and effectiveness. 'Councillors need tools to work strategically. They need to understand what will change the game and the big levers to pull

to benefit their community. Role clarity helps Councillors, the Council executive, and operational staff understand their various strategic roles.'

Local government has a unique and complex governance–management relationship, which risks creating an almost adversarial dynamic between Councillors and officers. Opportunities to build shared purpose and understanding between the two arms without the scrutiny of the media and community are rare but extremely valuable. Choosing to focus on the relationships within and between governance and the executive has paid dividends for Mildura.

Mayor Wood says, 'Council staff and Councillors are the closest I've seen in my three years in Council. The relationship is so strong that Councillors will fiercely defend Council staff. And many people I've spoken to who've been here longer than me say the same thing. Breaking down those barriers through open dialogue has been really good for the organisation. One of the best things was it brought the team closer. We learned more about each other, and while we have our differences, we can work positively together.'

In a collaborative environment like Council, decisions are as much about how people work together as it is about the decisions made. With a strong relationship, Council feels more confident making bold choices. Mayor Wood says, 'Sure, there are many parameters in local government, but there's also flexibility. There's a lot of rules, but you can still make a difference.'

RELATIONSHIPS

Encourage productive disagreement
for faster progress.

08

From adversaries to allies

When I was 22 years old and a graduate policy analyst, I was assigned my first strategic planning assignment. The brief: prepare a 'Biodiversity Action Plan' for the district in collaboration with stakeholders, acting on the Council's behalf.

A working group with farmers, landowners, dairy and beef companies, environmental protection groups, national park rangers, and regional and central government staff members had been convened to agree on a shared plan.

I set to task with the starry-eyed enthusiasm of a fresh graduate, and through a series of meetings and workshops, we found our way.

On the face of it, it's a tricky task. The group's members had deeply entrenched positions and a lot at stake.

They had:

- Wildly different ideas about what mattered most – in particular, the tension between economic growth and environmental protection.

▌ Strong identities in their professional and personal roles – local farmers represented a long, multi-generational tradition of working the land for production. By the same token, unpaid activists had dedicated their lives to protecting native species.

This project taught me important lessons about facilitating a group with different ideas and strong identities. It also showed me people can reach a consensus even if they risk losing face on what matters most to them.

Here's the secret: alignment isn't agreement. It's *productive disagreement*. Practical alignment, which brings diverse perspectives, values, and communities together, is about productively disagreeing to reach a consensus.

Every community is a rich tapestry of ideas, beliefs, experiences, and perspectives – not right or wrong, but different. Representative local democracy brings those differences to decisions to incorporate them into important choices that shape your place. When those differences appear at the Council table, we don't want them eliminated, proven wrong, minimised, or glossed over. We want them heard, celebrated, and meaningfully incorporated into our decisions.

With the Biodiversity Action Plan, I learned that reaching consensus requires more than simply presenting compelling evidence.

People think our beliefs are based on evidence, but we're generally wrong. Facts do not change feelings.

Facts do not change feelings.

Proving someone wrong is not the path to alignment. Instead of focusing on where they diverged, the group made progress at the level of abstraction where they converged – purpose, values, and shared narrative. At that level, everyone can be right without getting their own way.

Once we elevated our conversation to convergence, we broke through. Everyone in the room had a deep respect for and connection to the land and a strong desire to preserve it for future generations, whether for farming, recreation, or species preservation. Once the group focused on what they might gain, not lose, they developed a set of shared principles. They were adversaries until they became allies.

RELATIONSHIP ISSUES

Conflicting values and different thinking are normal and important in a diverse community, and the Council is no exception. In fact, high conflict can be an enabler of good governance rather than a barrier.[28] Perspective diversity strengthens the collaborative process, especially for the high-ambiguity, complex, and long-term decisions that Council leaders engage in.[29]

The difficulty with diversity is not that people think, feel, or act differently. The problem is when people become trapped in what academics call a 'social psychology of antagonism'[30] – in other words, it becomes about 'us vs them'. When Councillors are at war and the governance–management relationship is tense, Council and the community suffer.

In adversarial Councils:

- Big decisions are slow and painful.
- Meetings and workshops are long and frustrating.
- You feel isolated from your colleagues and peers.
- Officers pursue separate goals and priorities to elected members.
- Information is massaged and censored.

---

28 Ansell & Gash, 2008a.
29 Olson et al., 2007; Simons & Peterson, 2000.
30 Ansell & Gash, 2008b.

- Negative press, social media barbs, and antagonism affect public trust.
- Arguments and conversations are repeated, and decisions are relitigated.
- Decisions are escalated unnecessarily.
- People engage in alliance-building behind closed doors.

Local government is a relationship game. Practically speaking, few decisions can be made alone. The most important ones must be made as part of a negotiated process with your community, colleagues, and stakeholders. The quality of those decisions is largely determined by how well you work together with other decision-makers.[31]

In this section

Relationships are a critical shift for local government leaders to make faster, better decisions for the long-term benefit of their community.

In this section, we will explore:

- Common relationship challenges.
- The three building blocks of good relationships.
- Practical interventions to support the relationships shift.

RELATIONSHIP CHALLENGES

Two challenges make collaborative relationships uniquely difficult within and between governance and management in local government: role blurring and fragmented politics.

When these factors aren't managed, Councils get stuck in a vicious cycle of mistrust and antagonism.

---

31 Christensen et al., 2018.

Role blurring

In Weber's classic model of the political-administrative relationship, governance and management are clearly divided. Politicians develop visions, goals, policies, and strategies for administrators to implement.[32] However, reality is more complex, especially in local government. Administrators are often involved in setting direction, and politicians tend to become involved in individual community cases.[33]

The nature of the problems local government tackles – values-based, complex, wicked problems that no one actor can tackle alone and where no uniquely perfect solution can be found – requires interdependency and a blurring of roles. This overlapping and networked relationship can be hard to marry with role definition, and the lines between governance and management blur quickly, making it hard to set the terms for meaningful collaboration.

Fragmented politics

The governance–management relationship in local government is uniquely antagonistic. It's uncommon to find Boards and organisations so suspicious of one another in any other sphere. A corporate executive would rarely perceive their Board as a threat, nor would the Board accuse company employees of acting against their customers' interests.

Local government is unique in the public sector. Conflict is common in state, federal or national government, but it is usually at the party level – and criticising public servants is frowned upon.

These boundaries largely evaporate at the local level, whereparty politics are rare. People are individually elected, often to a particular ward, in what amounts to a coalition of one-person political parties. Individual Councillors are pitted against each other, and

---

32   Hansen & Ejersbo, 2002.
33   Ibid.

some elected members also agitate against the administration. This dynamic, unique to local government, is a recipe for toxicity.

RELATIONSHIP TRANSFORMATION

Nothing in local government happens alone. By law, all meaningful decisions are made in public or with the public. In a practical sense, local government leaders do not have the luxury of mucking around with petty politics. They're too broke, too stretched, and have too many important problems that require their attention to waste time playing games.

I believe the single most predictive determinant of a Council's effectiveness is the quality of the relationship between, first, the Mayor and the Chief Executive; second, the Councillors; and third, the broader Councillor group and the executive team.

When governance and management collaborate effectively, the potential for progress is unlocked. Under these conditions, Councils and communities thrive. Elected members clarify a strategic vision, build community connections, make critical decisions, and advocate for local interests. Executive managers enable the organisation to deliver on political and community outcomes.

The pull toward adversarialism is strong. But when Councils, already at a financial, legal, and logistical disadvantage, don't collaborate, they leave public value on the table. Truly impactful local government leadership demands quality relationships.

When you collaborate productively, your Council will:

- Make faster, more confident decisions.
- Speak more freely and frankly without fear.
- Produce fewer, better, shorter, and clearer reports.
- Enjoy shorter, more satisfying meetings and workshops.

- Save time and energy by avoiding unnecessary tasks and issues.
- Achieve fulfilment and purpose by excelling in your unique role.
- Build a strong support network to help you overcome challenges.
- Eliminate political game-playing and whispers.

Choose to be allies, not adversaries, and enjoy the speed and performance that a unified, aligned, high-trust governance–management dynamic can offer.

The three building blocks of productive relationships

There are three building blocks to productive relationships within and between elected members and executive managers:

1. Reliance.
2. Role clarity.
3. Respect.

Chapter 8 summary

- High conflict can enable good governance, but role-blurring and fragmented politics create mistrust and antagonism.
- Effective local governance relies on productive collaboration between mayors, councillors, and executives.
- Collaborative relationships lead to faster decisions, reduced political games, and stronger community trust.
- Relationships in local government hinge on reliance, role clarity, and respect among leaders.

09

Reliance

'Change moves at the speed of trust.'

Stephen M. R. Covey

Councillors are often surprised when I tell them how scary it is to present at a Council meeting. For officers who've poured their time, effort, and expertise into a report for approval, it feels like elected members have all the power. To make matters worse, many of these conversations happen before the public and media, where officers can be shamed, discredited, or questioned for their integrity or competence.

Councillors can be unwittingly antagonistic for similar reasons. Trying to interpret and respond to a technical report outside of your expertise is overwhelming, especially if you've been elected to make good decisions and hold the institution to account. Because officers are the experts who spend the money, manage projects, and implement policies, Councillors can feel like confused and powerless rubber stampers.

Managers have the knowledge and information, while Councillors have the power and control the resources. When we marry those asymmetries productively, they become complementary checks and balances. When tension and mistrust develop, they become frustrating roadblocks.

Even the most cautious driver slows down with a police car in their rear-view mirror. Similarly, even the most diligent public servant will develop fear and defensiveness when reporting to a suspicious Council. Faced with this defensiveness, committed politicians develop anxiety and suspicion that they are not receiving the full truth. Local government relationships are set up for trouble, and this adversarial dynamic can quickly become toxic without intervention.

The system works best when we acknowledge and work with the asymmetries in the governance–management relationship.[34]

With power comes responsibility. Because managers have the information and expertise, they are responsible for providing transparent, robust, digestible, synthesised, and material information. Because Councillors can interrogate and decide, they are responsible for asking questions that assume positive intent, respect expertise, put curiosity before cynicism, and draw connections. When managers provide great information, and Councillors ask great questions, conflicting asymmetries can become a collaborative advantage.

Councillors and Council managers rely on each other to do their job effectively. Neither can progress without the other, so mutually beneficial, interdependent relationships will enable better outcomes for projects, the Council, and the community.

---

34 Ansell & Gash, 2008a.

Three building blocks of relationships

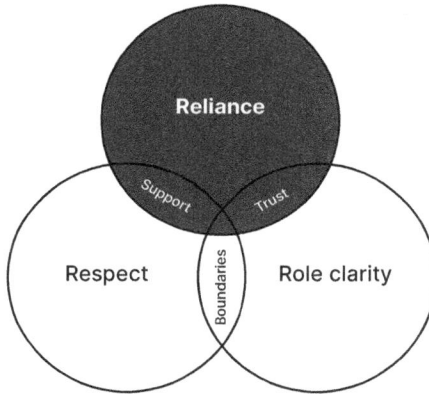

TRUST

According to Patrick Lencioni, an absence of trust is the most severe dysfunction a team can have.[35] If people don't trust each other, they waste time and energy protecting themselves and undermining each other instead of working on shared goals.[36] Mistrust slows progress.

Trust drives performance. Problems are solved faster when opinions feel safe to share. Meetings are quicker when people trust each other to deliver. Airport security scanning is twice as fast when security staff trust people to comply.[37] Everything is simpler and easier without layers of protective bureaucracy.

But trust can be hard to come by.

This isn't just a local government issue. Trust is low across the board. Declining social trust, seen in the rise of sovereign citizen groups

---

35   Lencioni, P. M., 2002.
36   Ibid.
37   Covey, Stephen M. R., 2006.

like My Place, impacts local government's social license and creates tension in Council relationships.

When we have a strong foundation of trust, everything gets easier. High trust speeds up key decision processes, makes negotiations more efficient[38], simplifies dispute resolution[39], and enables us to adjust more quickly to environmental changes[40].

Two types of trust

There are two main types of trust: 'competence-based trust' and 'integrity-based trust'. Competence-based trust expects our partner to have the skills and experience needed to do a good job, but integrity-based trust assesses their honesty, motives, and character.[41]

People assess and treat these two dimensions of trust differently, and one carries more weight than the other.

We forgive a performance breach because of someone's character, but we don't forgive an integrity breach because of someone's competence. If we want to rely on one another, we should prioritise integrity-based trust because it is 10 times more effective at reducing transaction costs than competence-based trust.[42]

> ## We don't forgive an integrity breach because of someone's competence.

In professional environments, leaders usually focus on building competence-based trust. Unfortunately, no amount of competence will mend an integrity fracture.

---

38 Das & Teng, 1998.
39 Poppo & Zenger, 2002.
40 Hitt, Ahlstrom, Dacin, Levitas, & Svobodina, 2004.
41 Connelly et al., 2018.
42 Connelly, B. L., Crook, T. R., Combs, J. G., Ketchen, D. J., & Aguinis, H., 2018.

Tense political conditions naturally tend toward low trust. In low-trust conditions, uneasy Councillors will seek more information and input, and defensive managers deliver detailed reports and technical assessments. This slows down decisions and performance. The forces driving Councils toward adversarial dynamics make integrity-based trust particularly important.

How to build trust within and between governance and the executive

The research is clear: trust is built with dedicated face-to-face dialogue.[43] When local government leaders within and across the political–administrative divide spend regular time together discussing areas of shared importance, they build a foundation of commitment and understanding. In short, they begin to trust each other.

Regular time together exposes us to the daily realities of others, making it easier to understand each other's pressures and perspectives and to trust in their intentions. Over time, that incremental trust-building creates a foundation of reliance and respect, supporting a virtuous cycle of trust and progress.

Schedule Councillor-only and governance-management time to build trust

Building trust requires more than competence. We need a personal connection to believe the other person acts with integrity. Schedule Councillor-only and governance-management time outside formal meetings to create opportunities to build integrity-based trust. The bonds of trust you build in these forums will speed up formal deliberation and decisions.

---

43   Ansell & Gash, 2008a.

SUPPORT

In a perfect world, there would be crystal-clear delineation between the roles of elected members and Council officers.

Politicians would set policy goals and objectives, and bureaucrats would implement these policies efficiently and impartially. The political and administrative functions would be neatly divided, and everyone would have the time, skills, and resources to do their job well.

In the real world, everyone is stretched and struggling. We depend on each other to do our jobs well. It is critical for Councillors and Council managers to support each other.

How politicians and administrators can support each other

Local government leaders don't have time and money to waste. They must rely on each other, which requires a strong foundation of integrity-based trust and a commitment to genuine support.

With few exceptions, elected members are not professional politicians but part-time amateurs juggling competing commitments. They rely on their administration differently than politicians in other tiers of government. In the same vein, Council officers depend on Councillors, for different reasons – release of funding and policy support, and sometimes, protection from the media and irate stakeholders!

Instead of ignoring these realities, strategic Councils embrace the interdependence of their respective roles and support each other.

Make each other's job easier

Officers should seek ways to reduce stress, streamline decisions, and make decision-making clearer and simpler for Councillors.

Reports, workshops, committee processes, scheduling, and Council information often have room for much-appreciated improvement.

Councillors should seek ways to reduce fear, confusion, and overwhelm from Council officers. Learning and using the correct Council processes, reading Council papers ahead of time, and speaking about officers with respect go a long way.

Chapter 9 summary

- Reliance requires trust and support.
- There are two types of trust: competence-based and integrity-based trust.
- Integrity-based trust is the most important for performance and progress.
- Councils can build integrity-based trust with dedicated face-to-face time.
- Councillors and Council managers should support each other and seek ways to make each other's jobs easier.

10

Role clarity

Councils across Australia and New Zealand lack role clarity. Without clarity, we risk overlap and oversight. Some jobs are left undone, while others are overdone. This leads to wasted time, accumulated resentment, and overall confusion, which can kill productivity and progress.

When we're clear on where our roles start and end, we don't limit ourselves – we open the door to innovation and excellence. In Councils with clear roles, elected members focus on setting direction and connecting with their colleagues. Executive managers facilitate quality decisions and organisational alignment, while Council managers oversee quality service delivery.

Three building blocks of relationships

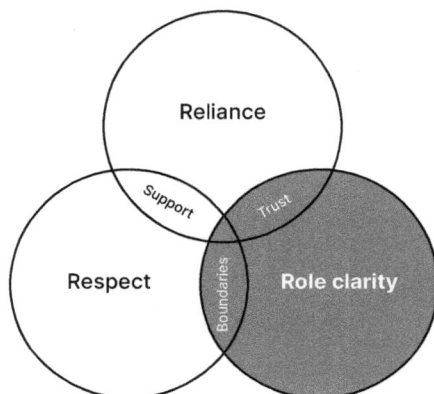

Reliance

Support

Trust

Respect

Boundaries

Role clarity

THE ELECTED MEMBER ROLE

Councillors are elected to represent and advocate for the needs and interests of their community at the highest local level. They have the privilege of direct connection to the people they serve, but that connection has downsides. They hear many frustrations and complaints, and the short-term problems seem endless.

Most Councillor inductions are like lessons for naughty schoolchildren – focused on what they aren't allowed to do. Councillors are rarely provided with useful job descriptions to understand their role or direct their energy meaningfully. Council meeting time is precious, and few opportunities exist to build productive working relationships. When you combine limited relationship-building and skill development time with 24/7 community availability and visibility, it's easy to see why role clarity is so difficult.

With confusing boundaries, competing demands, complex processes, unclear direction, and complicated relationships, Councillors committed to serving their constituents often take on individual service requests and complaints.

But the Council is more than a service provider – if bins, roads, and footpaths were the most important things, we wouldn't bother with elections. The most important part of a Councillor's role is democracy, not utility. When Councillors embrace their democratic role, get behind collective efforts for change, and support strategic planning[44], outcomes shift.

> ## The most important part of a Councillor's role is democracy, not utility.

The four critical jobs of a Councillor

Here are the four critical roles of an elected member:

1. *Future visionary.* Council creates public value, now and in the future. Councillors see the big picture and even the playing field, safeguarding public values like the environment, local character, and the health and well-being of the community. Elected members set and coordinate an aspirational vision for the future.

2. *Community advocate.* Councillors are a vital connection point between the community and the Council's decision-making and operational arms. They ensure a full range of voices are heard. Councillors understand what matters to people, so they can advocate on their behalf.

3. *Board member.* As governors, Councillor oversight ensures the Council administration runs fairly, efficiently, and effectively. They employ and manage the Chief Executive and stay apprised of big-picture organisational strategy, performance, and risk.

---

44   Vandersmissen, L., & George, B., 2023.

4. *Change-maker.* Councillors can change the rules and structures that shape community life. They can do this directly through policy change in their Council, and influence further afield by lobbying and engaging with government.

> **Support Councillors to embrace their role as community leaders**
>
> Positively focus Councillor induction on what elected members can do and influence before going deep on compliance, and legal and policy frameworks.
>
> Provide a clear role description with examples and guidelines and create supporting guidance for what to do and say when faced with a constituent request, conflict of interest, or other issue.

THE EXECUTIVE MANAGER ROLE

Senior local government managers are uniquely visible and connected to the public. They face the public and media at Council and community meetings, manage stakeholder relationships, and are often called in to solve operational crises. The connection and responsiveness expected of the Council's executive team is incomparable to many other sectors or tiers of government.

Many executive managers have a long career history as subject matter experts, particularly in smaller and non-metropolitan Councils. They're used to knowing the answers and are often put on the spot in public.

These pressures make it difficult to shift executive managers out of operational thinking and into strategic leadership – but for strategic Councils, facilitative, process-focused leadership is the most effective role an executive manager can play.

Executive managers are the meat in the strategy sandwich, facilitating upstream (to support decisions and direction from elected members) and downstream (to enable the delivery of projects, services, and work programmes). They are systems leaders, designers, and enablers, creating the conditions for others to perform at their best and removing barriers to progress.

> Executive managers are the meat in the strategy sandwich, facilitating upstream and downstream.

The three key jobs of an executive manager

When executive leaders see themselves as stewards of the decisions[45] and delivery, Councils work more effectively and deliver better outcomes. This involves three key roles for Council managers:

1. *Facilitator.* Executive managers continuously negotiate conflicting values, agendas, and ideas with the people around them – managing skirmishes, complaints, decisions, conversations, and consultation processes with stakeholders, staff, and Councillors. Executive managers need the skills to generate ideas, keep conversations moving, mediate conflict, and build consensus.[46]

2. *Systems leader.* As systems leaders, executive managers remove friction at the point where governance and operations intersect. They interrogate group dynamics and interactions, mend connection points, and design organisational systems and environments to enable others to succeed. As system

---

45   Chrislip, D. D. L. & Carl E., 1994.
46   Luke, J. S., 1998.

integrators, they bring planning and execution together[47], removing structural, policy, and process barriers and releasing resources where needed.

3. *Translator.* Executive managers are the golden thread that holds the decision and delivery arms of the Council together. As the connection point between politicians and the administration, senior leaders speak both languages. Executive managers translate big-picture vision into organisational design and organisational issues into strategic recommendations. They translate strategic priorities into planning documents, communications, budgets, work programmes, and projects, then translate those into clear, concise reports for Councillors.

Support managers to become collaborative facilitators

Agree, as an executive team, on your role as enablers and facilitators. Create a set of question prompts for your meetings that encourage this thinking.

For example:

- Are there structural or policy factors we should address?
- Which relationships are involved and how are they working?
- How can we bring others together to tackle this problem or meet this opportunity?

LEVERS FOR STRATEGIC IMPACT

It's easy for all local government leaders, elected or executive, to become tangled in Council processes and procedures or be sucked into the details of technical reports and community service requests. This is a recipe for frustration, overwhelm, and cynicism.

---

47 Bryson, J., Crosby, B., & Barberg, B., 2023.

Pull the right levers, and local government leaders can have tremendous impact.

Elected members can be incredible community advocates and change-makers. They can shape the lives of their community, now and into the future – provided they remember the strategic choices at their disposal and avoid getting stuck in the nitty-gritty.

Executive managers, when they stop thinking of themselves as experts and begin to think of themselves as enablers, can transform the pace and ease of progress at the political and administrative levels.

When in doubt, elected members and executive managers should focus on the three Rs: rules, resources, and relationships.

Rules

Councillors influence policy and legislation through review committees, collaboration with Council staff, and engagement with higher tiers of government. Elected members frustrated with a particular decision or outcome should redirect that frustration toward the rules that enabled it: What policy, process, or procedure is involved? What opportunity is there to change?

Executive managers influence, direct, and shape organisational policies and processes. When performance lags, managers should redirect their frustration from the people involved toward organisational design: How is work allocated across this department? How does information flow between people and teams? Is the guidance clear? Are organisational priorities clear and embedded?

Change the rules

Review the policies and processes that underpin outcomes you dislike. This widens your impact and leaves things better than you found them.

Resources

Councillors hold the purse strings. Influencing the overall allocation of community resources is a powerful lever. A Councillor's contribution to resource allocation can ensure current and future priorities are met. Elected members should get involved with the 'why' behind the budget, not just line items and rates increases.

Executive managers can direct and release funds within the organisation, purchase and approve additional resources and capabilities such as people, plant, and technology, and empower managers to act within their financial delegations. Focusing on how resources are used to achieve Council and community goals is more powerful than fiddling at the edges.

> **Put your money where your mouth is**
>
> If you're dissatisfied with how things are, follow the money. Change the way resources are allocated to prioritise what matters most.

Relationships

Councillors are key community connection points. Building strong relationships opens the door to partnerships with interest groups, industry, and government agencies. This is a great way to make shared progress on complex community issues that the Council cannot solve alone. Elected members should engage widely and deeply with the community through consultation, public meetings, and attendance at key events. They can also use the media for good, raising awareness of new and emerging issues facing the community and educating on how the Council can help.

For executive managers, relationships are just as critical. Forging relationships within, across, and outside the organisation will build social capital and make facilitation and collaboration easier. Collaborating with peers, uniting for sector advocacy, partnering with business and government, and connecting teams are all powerful ways to make progress.

Put people first

Prioritise relationships to create leverage and tackle tricky problems together. Two heads (and wallets) are usually better than one.

Chapter 10 summary

▌ Role clarity will drive greater impact but is difficult due to the interdependence of local government.

▌ Elected members are guardians of the future, community advocates, Board members, and change-makers.

▌ Senior leaders are facilitators, systems leaders, and translators.

▌ Both parties should focus on three levers for strategic impact: rules, resources, and relationships.

11

Respect

*'When we fail to set boundaries and hold people accountable,
we feel used and mistreated. This is why we sometimes
attack who they are, which is far more hurtful than
addressing a behavior or a choice.'*

Brené Brown, *The Gifts of Imperfection*

I've only ever had one group of Councillors refuse to return to a workshop with me, and it was because I said they couldn't chase up pothole complaints.[48]

The closest I'd come to walkout status before then was in the deep South of New Zealand when, overcome with frustration at a Councillor, I blurted out, 'Why don't you just keep a bucket of bitumen in your boot? You can fix the potholes yourself while you're driving around!' That time, there was a stunned pause in the room before we all burst into laughter. Phew.

---

48 Okay, there's slightly more to it than that. I got into a toe-to-toe with a long-serving Councillor, which culminated in me telling her she was actively perpetuating inequality by giving certain community members privileged access to power. This was not my finest moment as a facilitator! But I stand by the principle.

I have more tact now, but these conversations are still tense – and for good reason. Councillors face constant bombardment from constituents about perceived service failures. From a place of genuine care, they do their best to serve, support, and hold the administration accountable, so they interfere.

Councillors aren't the villains here, nor are Council managers. Getting these relationships right is hard work for local government leaders, but politicians and administrators are too interdependent to allow antagonism to fester. Bringing respect to Council relationships requires boundaries.

Three building blocks of relationships

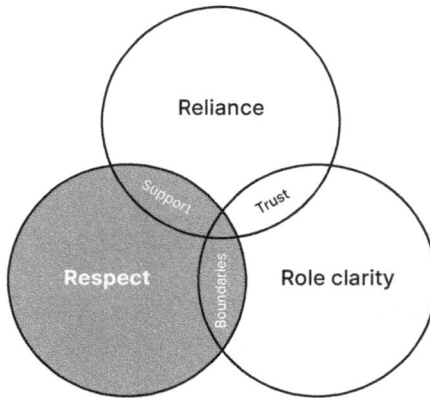

BOUNDARIES

Local government leaders are uniquely accessible to the public. We wouldn't expect to call Telstra and speak directly to the Chief Executive or Chairperson about our phone connection, nor do we expect to speak with the Prime Minister about our passport delay. None of those people would think it reasonable to respond to our questions personally. Yet, in a community setting, with people we know and problems we understand, the lines blur.

When the lines between operational and political blur too far, Councillors are hamstrung from doing what they've been elected to do, and executive managers can't do their job properly either.

Boundaries ensure everyone can do the job they're meant to be doing. Maintaining boundaries between governance and management allows each party to develop a healthy and reliable bond of mutual dependence.

Common boundary issues in local government are:

- Operational intervention by Councillors and executive managers to address minor issues and service requests.
- Strategic planning by Council managers that crosses into governance territory.

Both boundary issues reinforce the other and have the potential to create a vicious reinforcing cycle of mistrust and overstepping.

Common boundary issue 1: Operational intervention for minor issues and service requests

For many community members, the Council is an amorphous bureaucratic blob, from the dog control officer to the Mayor. When they complain about potholes, barking dogs, overhanging trees, or uneven footpaths, they may contact their local Councillor instead of using the customer service process.

These requests should be redirected to the administration, but Councillors, keen to help and concerned about organisational performance, interfere with or circumvent the formal process. This can cause confusion and frustration for staff, elected officials, and the community.

Constituents become confused about who is responsible for addressing their concerns and are frustrated when they receive inconsistent responses. The inconsistency and privileged access to Councillors for a lucky few undermines the integrity of Council services to the whole community and compromises established decision processes.

Interference leads to inefficiency, as some enquiries are double-handled, and more important requests get bumped down the queue. This ad-hoc approach and the expectation of instant or urgent turnaround create delay, disorganisation, and overload for operational teams.

Trust breaks down when Councillors undermine operational staff by bypassing formal processes.

Write the script

Create clear guidance for Councillors and staff about managing customer issues and requests that don't come via the correct channels. Provide templates and scripts to support this.

Common boundary issue 2: Strategic planning becomes corporate planning

Local government planning and reporting are increasingly regulated by higher tiers of government, placing pressure on already strained teams. Planning and reporting are full-time, year-round jobs. This compliance overhead weakens the democratic character of community planning. Financial reporting requirements and performance measures take centre stage, marginalising the democratic role and creating a void of contribution.

In a New Public Management (NPM) paradigm, strategic planning becomes corporate planning. Plans, budgets, targets, and metrics become the core focus, prioritising short-term gains over inter-generational progress, outputs over outcomes, and efficiency over effectiveness. This planning style leaves little room, attention, and respect for the Councillor's role in shaping a long-term strategy for their community.

Corporate and community leadership are not the same. However, when democratic governance is not well explained or enabled, Councillors default to what gets the most attention: corporate leadership. Rather than grappling with difficult political issues and community trade-offs, elected members focus on operational details: projects, budget lines, and targets. Senior officers then take on a democratic role, preparing the broader strategic direction and trade-offs.[49]

Frustration builds on both sides. Officers resent Councillors for not owning the plan, and Councillors resent officers for making decisions and spending money that elected members will be held accountable for.

When Councillors are empowered to own their democratic role, they don't meddle. They're too busy setting direction, advocating for their community, and building relationships.

When Councillors are empowered to own their democratic role, they don't meddle.

It's difficult and time-consuming to push beyond the legislative constraints of strategic planning and enable Councillors to own the big-picture direction. This requires facilitative and governance skills from senior Council officers.

Facilitate democracy

Prioritise Councillor engagement in the big-picture strategic framework of your next medium-term plan and be careful about letting the wrong things take priority.

Build facilitation skills among senior officers for more meaningful and productive strategic planning conversations.

---

49   Sullivan et al., 2006

GUIDELINES

Boundaries are values on legs. Establishing boundaries encodes respect in Council operations, which requires systems, policies, and processes.

Boundary systems

Create effective systems to support boundaries through governance policies and processes, internal systems and technologies, and guidelines and templates for staff and Councillors.

> **Changes to implement effective boundaries between Councillors and managers include:**
>
> - Co-created codes of conduct and terms of reference within and between governance and management groups, which include specific examples and guidance for managing questions, issues, or concerns.
> - Guidance material for induction and beyond, to explain how different laws, policies, and strategies fit together, and the opportunities for elected member involvement.
> - A policy review schedule, published months in advance, and guidance about how and when Councillors can contribute to the review process.
> - Scripts, templates, and guidance for Councillors to manage community requests fairly and consistently.
> - Early-engagement strategic planning processes that create time, space, and guidance for meaningful elected member leadership.

QUALITY QUESTIONS

'Judge a man by his questions rather than by his answers.'

Voltaire

Council meetings and workshops can become disrespectful because of the pressure placed on the interactions, fear of being fooled, and public performance. In this environment, questions become sly smokescreens for accusations and frustration.

A powerful way to demonstrate respect is to ask quality questions free of judgement, blame, or ulterior motives. In public forums, this can be more difficult than it sounds. Even innocuous-sounding questions ('Can we explain the delays on ... ') are often traps.

Quality questions do four things: assume positive intent, put curiosity first, serve the room, and keep it clean.

Assume positive intent

Assume everyone is motivated by good and doing their best. This is almost always true, and even when it isn't, we still get better results by making a positive assumption. This may require some internal dialogue and slow breathing.

Put curiosity first

Seek first to understand, then be understood. If the answer was as obvious as it looks, they would have already solved it. Assume there's something you don't know and be open to hearing about it.

Serve the room with open questions

Don't ask questions that only solve one issue. Level up your questions to identify underlying causes, systemic barriers, and overall trends. Expanding your scope multiplies your impact.

Keep it clean

No 'gotcha' moments. If you ask a question to try to trick someone into admitting they've made a mistake or proving something you've already decided, that's not a question. It's an accusation.

***

Quality questions transform governance and management interactions. When everyone comes in with an open mind, kind tone and curious approach, progress is faster, easier, and much less frustrating.

Chapter 11 summary

▍ Respect requires clear boundaries.

▍ Two common boundary issues in local government are operational intervention for minor issues and service requests and strategic planning, which becomes corporate planning.

▍ Operationalise respect through systems, policies, and quality questions.

Relationships in practice

'The truth will set you free, but first it will piss you off.'

Gloria Steinem

How well you work together is more important than how good you are at your job. In local government, a group of all-star thinkers who don't make decisions or trust each other is largely impotent.

Your collaborative competence delivers more than the sum of its parts. Think of it like an infinite loop. Each part of the strategy system has a role, which depends on input and cooperation from the other parts. The lines sometimes blur, but we make positive progress with reliance, role clarity, and respect.

PRODUCTIVE DISAGREEMENT

People will inevitably bring different perspectives to the decision process. This isn't an obstacle to be overcome, especially for strategic and highly complex decisions. Disagreement enhances decision quality.[50] The more complex a decision is, the more useful it will be to orchestrate conflict – provided we ensure our conflict is focused squarely on ideas rather than identities.[51]

A healthy and productive working relationship does not require all parties to agree – remember alignment is not agreement. Alignment is productive disagreement. For senior leaders, too much agreement may indicate groupthink or that people aren't expressing their true opinions. We need competing ideas around the Council table, and building the skills for productive disagreement means people feel safe disagreeing with each other. Productive disagreement increases ownership and connection, for two reasons:

1. When you say your piece, you accept the outcome more readily

Well-meaning leaders and facilitators often avoid conflict or try to settle disagreements too quickly, assuming that dissent will weaken relationships and encourage disengagement.

Research suggests the opposite is true – a positive correlation exists between articulating your position and accepting decisions that affect you, even if your position does not prevail.[52] The discomfort generated by open disagreement is offset by an appreciation of shared knowledge and perspective that can be converted into a shared vision.

2. Relationship conflicts distract; reasoning conflicts enhance

Not all conflict is created equally. Conflicting ideas can hurt performance and outcomes at lower levels of an organisation, particularly in operational delivery. However, if there's trust, ideological conflict (expressed with respect) is almost always positive at the executive and governance levels.

---

50 Olson et al., 2007.
51 Simons & Peterson, 2000.
52 Ibid.

When we trust the people around us, we more openly challenge them without fear of recrimination or personal attack. Trust is crucial. Integrity-based trust makes it possible to show up with respect and assume positive intent of the other people involved. Competence-based trust makes it easier to disagree at an ideas level. If we believe the other person to be reliable, honest, *and* competent, we're more likely to engage in a war of ideas, not identities, increasing the quality of our decisions.[53]

RELATIONSHIP INTERVENTIONS

Trust is the biggest enabler of a healthy governance–management relationship. All relationships with potential conflict and misunderstanding need frequent, positive, meaningful connections, and the governance–management relationship is no exception.

The three conditions conducive to collaborative governance are reliance, role clarity, and respect. To improve relationships, focus on induction, recruitment, and trust-building.

Induction: start how you mean to continue

> 'Not everything that is faced can be changed,
> but nothing can be changed until it is faced.'
>
> James Baldwin

Few newly elected members understand how the Council works and their roles and responsibilities – particularly how demanding it will be.

An election focuses on arguments. But once elected, effectiveness needs alignment. The skills needed to be elected and rally public

---

53   Olson et al., 2007.

support are often the opposite of those needed to work well as a politician.

Council staff should circuit-break election behaviour early and lay the foundation with a great induction. Establish clear and shared expectations about behaviour and values as early as possible in the Council term. This code should apply between Councillors, between managers, and between Councillors and management.

Hit the ground running

- Be positive. Focus on all the great things Councillors can do, not just what they can't.
- Set the expectation for regular development time – in the first three months of the Council term and beyond.
- Create opportunities for relationship building within and between Council and the executive – away days, workshops, and shared development.

Recruitment: prioritise collaboration

Councils are like a family – we don't get to choose the other people involved, we're stuck with the consequences of their choices, and we won't get far without their cooperation. But unlike families, we have some input into who joins us at the table.

In candidate information evenings and pre-election briefings, emphasise the importance of relationships. Make it clear that the most effective political behaviour is collaborative, not competitive.

When recruiting leaders and Council officers, you have more sway. In job descriptions, interviews, and selection criteria, prioritise collaborative skills. Look for:

- *Attributes:* openness, outcome focus, passion, and humility.
- *Skills:* strategic thinking and facilitation skills.

Regardless of who joins you at the table, collaborative skills are learnable and coachable. You can always improve. If you engage with potential candidates pre-election, prioritise collaborative skills when hiring senior leaders, and build them through shared learning and development, you become an allied and collaborative Council.

Recruit for collaboration

- Emphasise the importance of collaboration with potential candidates pre-election.
- Prioritise collaborative and facilitation skills in job descriptions and recruitment processes.
- Invest in shared learning and development to build collaborative competence.

Build bonds of integrity-based trust

Spending quality time together will build integrity-based trust, the critical foundation for everything else. That can be hard to do in the confines of Council meetings, so the more informal time you have within and between governance and management teams, the better. Forums, workshops, away days, strategy sessions, and shared learning and development present opportunities to build bonds and trust.

Build trust

- Set up regular forums for councillors and staff to discuss ongoing issues, seek feedback, and share information outside formal Council meetings. This will build trust and promote mutual understanding.
- Develop clear and concise job descriptions that include the differences between governance and management. Staff and Councillor inductions and manuals are great for this.

▪ Establish a mentor programme where senior members guide newly elected Councillors through their new roles and responsibilities.

Chapter 12 summary

▪ Productive disagreement, centred on ideas rather than personal conflicts, enhances decision quality and fosters a culture of trust and respect.

▪ Building collaborative competence involves setting clear expectations, continuous development, and fostering informal interactions and trust-building activities.

▪ Prioritising collaborative skills in elections, recruitment, and training ensures a cooperative and effective Council.

Relationships in summary

- Relationships between elected and executive leaders are critical for local government, but the operating environment promotes an adversarial dynamic.

- Local government leaders face too many constraints to indulge in politics. Moving from adversaries to allies enables unity, efficiency, and performance.

- Two main relationship challenges to be aware of are:
    - Blurred lines between political and administrative roles can create a vicious cycle of suspicion and mistrust.
    - Fragmented politics encourage tension and attention-seeking.

- Relationships between governance and management in local government have three observable characteristics: reliance, role clarity, and respect.
    - Reliance requires trust.
    - Role clarity requires support.
    - Respect requires boundaries.

- Alignment is not agreement; it is productive disagreement.

- Asking quality questions will change conversations and relationship dynamics.

- Practical interventions to support the relationships shift include:
    - Job descriptions.
    - Recruitment priorities.
    - Positive and helpful inductions.
    - Regular and shared development.
    - Open forums and informal relationship-building time.

How the City of Mitcham transformed their annual planning and made better decisions

The City of Mitcham, in south Adelaide, has done an exceptional job building trust between the Council chamber and administration and establishing strategic decision frameworks since 2022, thanks to the dedication of Mayor Heather Holmes-Ross and CEO Matthew Pears. Mayor Holmes-Ross says, 'We were primed and ready for the conversation. I wanted us to be looking at things at a strategic level.'

CEO Matthew Pears says, 'It was an opportunity to go to the next level.' And go to the next level they did. Mitcham has streamlined communication and decisions, ensuring the right boundaries are in place. Newly elected Councillor Aidan Greenshields describes, 'We've agreed to delegate simple decisions that take up Council time. Staff are bringing less small stuff to us to keep us focused on the bigger, more important decisions.'

CEO Matthew Pears explains, 'Because we had that conversation with everyone in the room, we empowered the administration to make decisions they might not have made alone before.'

Mayor Holmes-Ross recalls, 'The process of going through our current strategic plan and weighting it was surprisingly easy.' Councillor Greenshields agrees. 'It was excellent. There wasn't bickering because it felt like we'd got there as a team.'

Applying their new strategic skills has transformed how Mitcham operates – including budgeting. Pears explains, 'Now we discuss options in terms of strategic alignment to our priorities – instead of

saying, "Here's our budget, what do we want to do with it?"' Councillor Greenshields adds, 'This year's budget process is about understanding whether a project is aligned with our priorities, then running it through our decision criteria. Is it the right thing, at the right time, for the right reason, with the right people?'

Framing their annual budgeting process around their strategy has helped Mitcham's elected members make wiser long-term decisions with resources. The new approach also makes Councillors responsible for assessing the strategic alignment of their budget requests, achieving consensus on that alignment, and negotiating prioritisation.

Once projects are shortlisted, the executive team assesses timing, resourcing, and logistics, giving Councillors expert advice so they can make holistic budget decisions. The transparency and accountability of this process have enabled and elevated City of Mitcham Councillors to strategic decision-makers for their whole community.

It's saved time, too. Pears recalls, 'The first Council meeting I attended ran for over 18 hours across three evenings. We used to have a meeting every two weeks. Now, we've gone to one meeting a month, and we're finishing that early.'

Once the ball got rolling, opportunities to systemise strategic decisions were everywhere. Pears says, 'We've stopped sending certain reports to elected members. The executive team make short-term decisions because they don't involve discussion on strategic direction. With long-term decisions, elected members need time and space to consider. We're giving Councillors more space for hundred-year decisions."

DECISIONS

Make more strategic decisions
for greater impact.

13

From operational to strategic

After four years, I left my Council job. I thought I might be happier in a commercial environment, so I went to work in a law firm. Where better to find pace and excitement than an environment billed in six-minute increments?

I lasted eight weeks.

I didn't mind the job, but the work/life balance was tricky. My husband and I had agreed to move our family to the city where my firm's head office was based. In the interim, I commuted an hour each way. I also travelled weekly to our other offices around New Zealand.

Working nights was common, and I saw little of my young children. I was juggling a patchwork of childcare arrangements and spent many nights in tears, wondering how to improve things.

Still, I was determined to hang on. The money was excellent, and I was the breadwinner since my husband had started a building apprenticeship. There was a lot on my shoulders. I also had something to prove – to myself and everyone who doubted me after I dropped out of school. Look at me now! I was 25 years old, had a company credit card, and had a great salary. I had made it.

But my values conflicted – professional success vs present parenting, financial safety vs fulfilling work. An imposter's voice whispered in my ear, too: surely this was a fluke – I wouldn't get an opportunity like this again.

In week eight, it was time to confirm our moving arrangements – schools for the kids, tenants for our home, and moving dates. We'd found somewhere in the city, and the rental agreement was in front of me, waiting to be signed. I was paralysed by indecision. Were we really going to make this move? Is this what we wanted?

I was good at the job. My boss only intended to stay for another two years and there was a path to promotion. But he worked even longer hours than I did. Looking to the future, it seemed like my work/life balance would get worse before it got better.

Finally, I permitted myself to consider other options. What if I … quit? Could we survive if I walked away from this job? With my husband on an apprentice wage, was there a way to pay our mortgage and get by? The sums didn't add up, but something shifted in me as I started to work on them. I wasn't sure what the solution was yet, but it became clear: I would leave the job.

Things moved swiftly after that. In just a few days, I went from fancy-pants career girl to stay-at-home Mum, with no idea what was coming next.

Fast-forward a decade, and most would consider this story to have a happy ending. We didn't go broke. I became a freelancer, then a consultant, and now have a successful business with international reach. I've found a way to do fulfilling work on my own terms while being there for my family.

But what if I hadn't? What if I'd not started my business, or failed at it, and never found another job that paid so well? Would it still have been the right decision to make? And what if I'd stuck at it a few more weeks or months in the job? Who's to say it wouldn't have gotten better?

What do you think?

Maybe you think it was the right decision because I was honouring my values: public service and time with my kids. Maybe you think it was the wrong decision because I was fickle. Maybe you are considering the alternatives – negotiating work hours with the law firm or returning to the Council.

Maybe you think there is no right decision regarding personal choices like this, or you want more information about the outcome to make a judgement call.

All those positions are fair and reasonable. This is one of those choices where everything is up for debate and discussion. No doubt you have faced such moments yourself.

DECISION SKILLS

In Council, you make decisions like my job dilemma: high stakes, conflicting values, multiple options, uncertain outcomes, and limited resources. These are *strategic decisions*, and unlike operational decisions, they are unlikely to have a correct answer. Everyone will have their own opinion about what matters most or which option to choose.

Strategic decisions can't be made by simply gathering more information or talking to the right expert. There are too many uncertainties and values involved. When everyone has a different point of view and a compelling case, it can feel impossible to make the right choice. The skills to make strategic decisions differ greatly from those used to make operational choices, and without these skills, Councils face huge challenges.

When local government leaders lack the skills to make strategic decisions, you get:

- Bottlenecks when reports can't get over the line.
- Relationship breakdowns over conflicting opinions.
- Decisions that contradict the Council's goals for the community.
- Long technical reports met with suspicion and distrust.
- Paralysis by analysis in the face of overwhelming issues and options.
- Wasted time spent debating options and choices that go nowhere.
- The presentation of 'done deals' to Councillors without room for meaningful input.
- Overambitious or unachievable plans with little to no prioritisation of key initiatives.

Strategic decisions aren't easy, and there is no foolproof prescription. You may – and often will – get them wrong. The good news is you make high-quality strategic decisions by focusing on the *process*, not the outcome, and alignment is more important than agreement.

> **Strategic decisions can't be made by simply gathering more information or talking to the right expert.**

In this section

In this section, we'll cover:

- The difficulties of strategic decisions.
- The elements of a good strategic decision.
- The three key stages of a strategic decision process.

- Why local government finds strategic decisions so difficult.
- Practical interventions and steps to support strategic decision-making.

DECISION DIFFICULTIES

Strategic decisions are difficult due to their uncertainty, subjectivity, and complexity.

Uncertainty

> *'There are no facts from the future.'*
> Carl Spetzler

Strategic decisions are not about facts and logic. First, they are about the future, which is always uncertain. Even the best historical information is still information about the past. Second, they often involve high significance and longer horizons, increasing ambiguity.

Strategic decisions require leaders to make tough calls even when clear, definitive information is lacking. This lack of clarity can lead to paralysis by analysis, where the fear of making the wrong decision outweighs the potential benefits of making any decision.

Uncertainty is particularly difficult in an interconnected environment. Investing in the Eiffel Tower changed the cultural narrative about Paris for the next century, created a multi-billion-dollar tourism industry, and permanently reshaped France's capital city. Modern Councils investing in green infrastructure have many uncertainties about future environmental regulations, technological advancements, and community acceptance. Decisions made in local government often have ripple effects that extend far beyond their immediate context.

Local government leaders are at the dual mercy of government and community change. They must grapple with multiple potential outcomes and be flexible and ready to adapt as new information and circumstances arise. They are asked to hold multiple behaviours in paradox: to be decisive but flexible, to maintain a long-term view but pivot as a situation evolves. This is a tall order for any leader.

Subjectivity

In 2019, Ashburton District Council proposed relocating a water fountain on the town's main street. They were scoping an upgrade of the area and planned to repatriate the 20-year-old fountain to the local domain. The community revolted, sparking an online petition that attracted over 1400 signatures and hundreds of furious comments. A few weeks later, the Council voted to leave the fountain where it was.

In 2021, the City of Darwin signalled its first bylaw review in over 30 years. Under the proposed bylaws, urban dwellers would be prohibited from keeping chickens except on land zoned for domestic livestock, and roosters would be banned on all non-rural land. Devastated chicken owners erupted at the Council. Writing on change.org, Elizabeth Clark asked: 'My beautiful chickens are just as much a part of my family as my children and grandchildren. Which child could you give up?'

After more than two years of negotiation, the Council reached a compromise: chickens (no more than six) could be kept on lots bigger than 600 square metres, at schools, and within rural living zones. A 12-month transition provided time for poultry owners to make alternative arrangements. In a press release, the Lord Mayor committed the Council to working with affected residents.

Some decisions we expect to be contentious or challenging due to their political connotations, but others can surprise us with their difficulty.

Making decisions that produce collective public value often requires trading values against one another. In my job decision, I traded financial safety and professional success against fulfilling work and present parenting. In the Eiffel Tower example, it was cultural and heritage preservation vs history-making – a trade-off many modern-day Councils face. For your Council, it might be economic growth against environmental protection or community safety against recreational opportunity. In all strategic decisions, subjectivity is rarely a matter of good over bad, but rather, which value to prioritise over another.

The more complex and strategic the issue, the more likely a value judgement will be required. The Council's ability to navigate value judgements fairly, transparently, and productively is a major determinant of how well a decision can be made.

Complexity

> 'Collaboration is not an easy answer to hard problems,
> but is instead a hard answer to hard problems.'
>
> Bryson et al., 2023

The public sector is criticised for being slow and underperforming compared to the private sector, but the evidence doesn't support this argument. According to an international literature review, there's no proof the private sector is any more efficient than the public sector.[54] When tackling problems like health and social care, electricity, water, transport, waste management, or telecommunications, the public and private sectors produce similar results.[55]

Addressing important social issues is more difficult and demanding than providing consumer goods and services. Professor Simon

---

54   European Public Service Union, 2019.
55   Ibid.

Collinson, creator of the Global Simplicity Index, discovered in 2012 that UK public sector organisations are 30% more complex than some of the world's largest companies.

This complexity is not due to inept bureaucrats but rather the nature of the work, the challenges to be resolved, and the demands of democracy. While operational decisions might be *complicated*, strategic decisions are often *complex*, with many moving parts and technical considerations. Local government isn't slow; it's tricky.

Local government isn't slow; it's tricky.

Despite all this, local government punches above its weight for delivery and cost-effectiveness.[56] In the last decade, while population size exploded and government services rapidly expanded, local government spending increased at a significantly slower rate than other tiers of government.[57]

The value of strategic decisions

> '*Right or wrong, decide. The road of life is paved with*
> *flat squirrels who could not make a decision.*'
>
> Anonymous internet meme

Uncertainty, subjectivity, and complexity make strategic decisions difficult but not impossible – and the payoff is worth the effort.

---

56 In Australia, Councils deliver almost a quarter of public services for less than 4% of total tax revenue.

57 SGS Economics and Planning, 2022. In Australia, between 2012 and 2021, while the Commonwealth's total outlays per capita grew by over 50% and state government outlays per capita increased by 32%, local government spending increased by just 23%, despite more exposure to population growth effects than the other tiers of government.

When local government leaders make better strategic decisions, you get:

- Faster, easier decision-making thanks to clear criteria and priorities.
- Healthy and productive discussions that respect differing opinions.
- Concise and readable reports that build trust and make it easier to grapple with uncertainty.
- Consistent and aligned decisions that support Council's goals for the community.
- Productive use of meeting time with focused discussions that lead to actionable decisions.
- More effective and meaningful engagement with a diverse range of voices.
- Achievable and well-prioritised plans that focus on key initiatives.
- Better services and outcomes for communities now, and in the future.
- More proactive decisions that safeguard Council and community well-being.

THREE COMPONENTS OF A DECISION

Good strategic decisions have three things in common. They are *full*, *fair* and *focused*:

- *Fullness* means we understand the context of our decisions and have considered all relevant elements. Fullness requires good questions.
- *Fairness* is about process and intent. Fairness requires integrity and awareness.

▌ *Focus* acknowledges the finitude of time, space, and resources, and provides criteria to maximise results within these limitations.

Chapter 13 summary

▌ Strategic decisions require different skills than operational decisions.

▌ Strategic decisions are difficult because of uncertainty, subjectivity, and complexity.

▌ Good strategic decisions are full, fair, and focused.

14

Fullness

*'If you're not making mistakes,
then you're not making decisions.'*

Catherine Cook

The ancient Indian parable about the blind men and the elephant has many permutations first appearing in a Buddhist text around 500 BCE.

In the story, a group of blind men encounter an elephant for the first time and inspect it by touch. Each man feels a different part of the elephant's body and draws a conclusion about the elephant's shape and form. The man who touches the trunk thinks an elephant is shaped like a snake. The man who touched the tail pronounced that elephants are like a rope. The man who fell against his side cried, 'The elephant is like a wall!', while the man who felt a tusk was sure an elephant was just like a spear.

Three components of a strategic decision

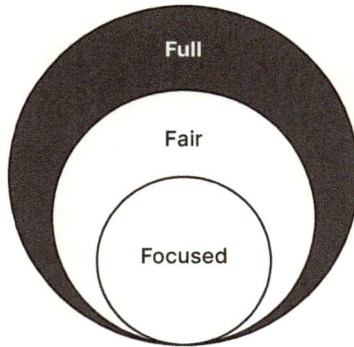

FULL INFORMATION

Humans draw broad conclusions based on limited, subjective experience. Like the blind men touching the elephant, if we draw conclusions too quickly or from a single perspective, we miss the big picture.

With strategic decisions, each new data point can change our position, so we need to get the full picture before we form an intuitive preference. Due to the uncertainty, subjectivity, and complexity involved, strategic decisions need quality information and context – and accessing that information depends on the quality of the questions we ask.

Our questions should attempt to touch every part of the elephant. One way Councils can do that is with the Right Decision Model.

In *You Don't Need An MBA*[58], I build on Greg McKeown's *Essentialism* model[59] to develop a comprehensive set of questions that examine different angles of an issue or decision. For strategic

---

58 McKay, A., 2021.
59 McKeown, G., 2014.

decisions in local government, these prompts strike the right balance of specific and subjective to provoke meaningful discussion.

The Right Decision Model checks all aspects of a decision, interrogating whether we have the right reason, right idea, right time, and right people. Missing one of these variables can compromise an otherwise promising decision. Let's break them down.

The Right Decision Model

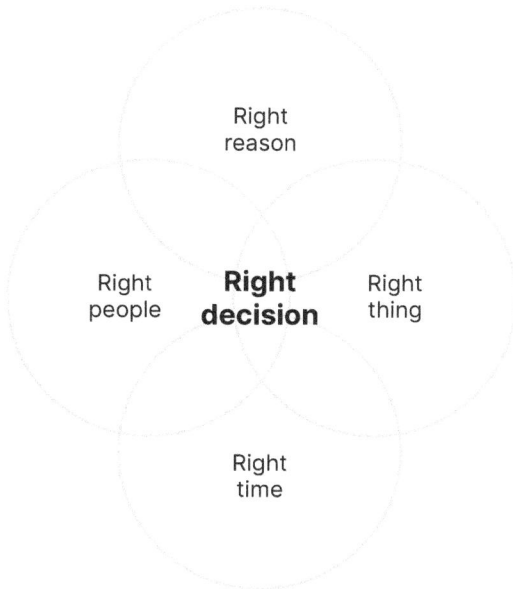

- *Right reason:* motivation and strategic alignment.
- *Right thing:* context, frame, options, and issues.
- *Right time:* readiness, connections, and dependencies.
- *Right people:* capabilities, influence, and relationships.

The right reason

There are lots of reasons to make a decision, but some reasons are 'right-er' than others. Beware of fear, pressure, obligation, or guilt. If there is any chance that this decision is about jumping on a band-wagon, scrambling for funding, pursuing status, or trying to buy our way out of a problem, pause.

Here is a list of reasons that might not prompt quality decision-making:

- Funding has become available (in an area where the Council had no significant projects planned).
- Councils across the state have all rolled out a new service, and there is pressure to keep up.
- There's an election coming, and this would be a popular project.

Checking for the right reason is a sense-check that involves honesty and interrogation. If we aren't motivated by the right drivers, it's hard to make the right choices.

> **To test the 'right reason', ask questions like:**
> - Why do we want to act on this now?
> - What has prompted this discussion?
> - What outcomes are we trying to achieve?
> - Are we being reactive or proactive?
> - Are we operating with integrity and alignment?
> - What are the costs and risks if we don't act?
> - Are we being honest with ourselves?

The right thing

The right idea is about more than the details of a given option. It is also about context – because our frame of understanding will change our available choices. Ensuring we understand a problem before hurtling head-first into solving it is critical in any decision.

People tend to solution-lock and then justify their choices retrospectively. We get a good idea, and it's all we can think about – even if we haven't given full thought to the nature of the problem we're solving and the full scope of options available. Maslow's Law of the Instrument rears its ugly head, and every new piece of information is further evidence for why our first idea is the right one.

Example: New sporting facility

The Council has built a new sporting facility on the east side of town. Low activity levels on this side of town prompted joint investment by the Council and state government. The state-of-the-art facility is open, but visits are much lower than expected.

Consultation with the community discovers some interesting facts:

- Many families on this side of town work irregular schedules, which do not align with the facility's opening hours.
- The new facility does not cater to the most popular sports among young people in this area (skateboarding and football). In fact, open space for football has now decreased, with the new building cannibalising the park area. The carpark and outdoor seating areas have proven popular with skateboarders ... who have been trespassed from the property due to safety concerns.

The Council was solving a problem, but it wasn't the right thing for the community it served. Better questions about the real problem being solved and more robust testing of plans with community members in this area might have led to a better outcome.

To determine whether we're focused on the right thing, we need to be aware of our context and the problem we're solving, as well as the suitability of the specific options being considered, if any.

To test the 'right thing', ask questions like:

- What is the real problem to be solved?
- Are we sure we understand the causes and consequences of this issue?
- Have we considered all our options?
- Have we done this before?
- Has this worked in other places?
- What would happen if we didn't do anything?
- How can we be sure this is the right course of action?

The right time

Plenty of failed inventions were ahead of their time. Microsoft invented a tablet a decade before Apple released the iPad, but it failed shortly after. AT&T developed a Picturephone in 1964, decades before Skype or FaceTime became popular, but the public, infrastructure, and supporting systems weren't ready for it. If you get your timing wrong, it doesn't matter how good your idea is.

Even if the timing seems right, the presence of other projects or external pressures could be cause for pause. You compromise your success if you roll out digital transformation directly after a restructure. If there's just been a natural disaster, it's coming into Christmas, or the economy has entered a recession, timing will help or hinder your outcomes.

More than enough problems are waiting to be solved, and few exist independently of each other. For this reason, our decisions must consider timing, dependencies, and sequencing.

To test the 'right time', ask questions like:

- Why now?
- What else is going on?
- Are we ready?
- Are they ready?

The right people

Many Council projects have gone awry because the right people weren't in the room or the Council didn't have the right skills, people, or influence to get the job done. This is particularly challenging in an environment where the Council can find itself the 'last resort' option for unpopular, infeasible, or challenging social initiatives.

Regardless of an idea's merit, timing, or reason, local government leaders must be keenly aware of their people limitations. The Council is not always the right actor to tackle a problem and can often worsen things. Nothing is more frustrating than failing to get the right people on your side. If you don't have the skills, capability, or mandate to act, you're set up for failure at the outset.

To test the 'right people', ask questions like:

- What capability is needed?
- Do we have the right skills?
- Who has the final say in this?
- How much influence do we have?
- Who else should be involved?
- Is Council the right organisation for the job?

***

This simple model allows your Council to adapt the criteria – what's 'right' to you? – to your unique circumstances and priorities. Group decision tools allow leaders to take a more comprehensive view of a decision and challenge their thinking respectfully without making a person or perspective 'wrong'. A decision can be right for one or more reasons and still be the wrong choice.

Warning: proceeding with a decision when one element is missing is risky. If one element is missing initially, more deficits are usually revealed with time.

Chapter 14 summary

- Strategic decisions need good information to avoid subjective biases and incomplete perspectives.

- Good information needs good questions.

- The Right Decision Model prompts questions about reason, thing, timing, and people, ensuring a well-rounded approach.

15

Fairness

'A good decision never turns bad, nor a bad decision good.'

Ron Howard

The Eiffel Tower could have been a disaster – plenty of ambitious infrastructure projects have been. For instance, decades after the completion of the Sydney Opera House, the jury is still out on whether the project was a success. Originally scoped as a $7-million-dollar project and expected to take four years, construction eventually cost over $100 million and took another decade to complete.

You might think the outcome – an iconic landmark for the city of Sydney – proves it was a good decision. This logic is known as 'resulting', where the quality of a decision is confused with the quality of its outcome.[60] We can't control luck, the law, the economy, or the environment, but we can focus on the integrity of our decision processes. This is especially important for long-term decisions where the outcome could be many decades away.

---

60   Duke, A., 2020.

It's like parenting – you do your best, cross your fingers, and don't find out for 25 years or more if it went okay. Even then, a subpar result might not be your fault. For that reason, good decisions are defined by the process we use to make them, not their outcome.[61] For local government decisions to be fair, leaders should focus on process and intent.

> **Good decisions are defined by the quality of their process, not the quality of their outcome.**

Three components of a strategic decision

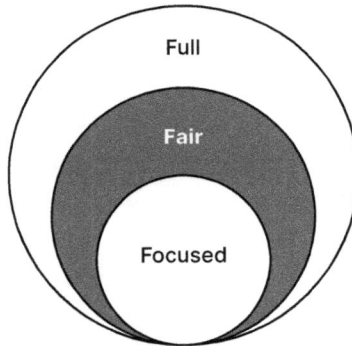

FAIR PROCESS

> *'Decision makers cannot use hindsight –*
> *that's a luxury for observers.'*
>
> Spetzler et al., 2016

---

61   Spetzler, C., Winter, H., & Meyer, J., 2016.

A strategic decision process has three key stages: building understanding, shaping choices, and making decisions.[62] If we pay attention to each stage and provide adequate time, space, and opportunity for engagement, we make high-quality decisions people are committed to.

In a Council, managers often handle the first two stages of the decision process before presenting a 'decision' to the Councillors. This is appropriate for operational matters but will not suffice for strategic decisions.

Let's dive into the three stages of a decision.

Three stages of a strategic decision

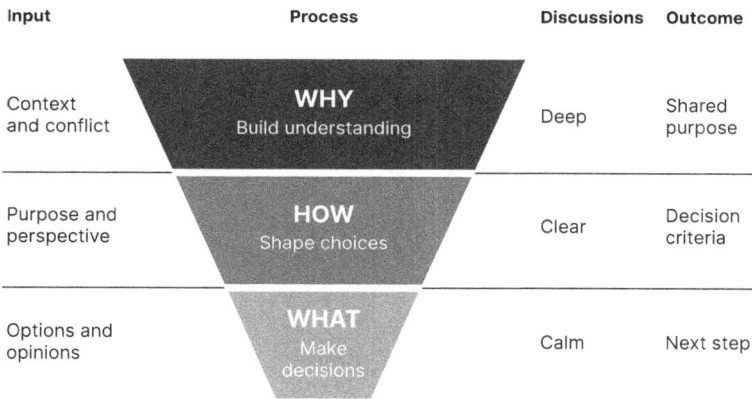

Input	Process	Discussions	Outcome
Context and conflict	**WHY** Build understanding	Deep	Shared purpose
Purpose and perspective	**HOW** Shape choices	Clear	Decision criteria
Options and opinions	**WHAT** Make decisions	Calm	Next step

Decision stage 1: Build understanding

We build understanding at the beginning of a decision, particularly if there is conflict or confusion. Building understanding features 'why' conversations that expand and enrich the context of the decision.

---

62 This framework is drawn from the facilitation handbook *Moments of Impact.* Ertel, C., & Solomon, L. K., 2014.

At this stage, we go deep, connecting decision-makers and affected parties to a shared purpose.

Building understanding requires gathering information, seeking diverse perspectives, and coming together for discussion. In this stage, decision-makers surface key viewpoints and challenges. This is also the time to orchestrate productive conflict. The more complex a decision is, the more useful disagreement is in improving the quality and ownership of the outcome.[63]

It is tempting to rush this decision stage but don't be fooled by the illusion of efficiency. Building understanding is like a slingshot. When people have the chance to be heard, they are significantly more likely to own the outcome of a decision.[64] An hour spent here can mean a month saved later.

Tips for building understanding

- Cast your information net far and wide, and bring in diverse stakeholders, studies, and sources. This prevents narrow framing too early in the process.
- For significant decisions, include Councillors and stakeholders at this stage.
- Ask decision-makers for their views anonymously and independently before coming together to discuss contentious issues. This ensures all voices are heard before the loudest and most confident ones take over.
- Do not rush into solving problems before hearing all views and perspectives.

---

63 Olson, B. J., Parayitam, S., & Bao, Y., 2007.
64 Simons, T. L., & Peterson, R. S., 2000.

Decision stage 2: Shape choices

When it's time to shape choices, we work at the 'how' to tighten criteria and interrogate options for change. The goal of these conversations is clarity.

Shaping choices is where decision-makers develop the criteria they will use to evaluate options. These criteria are based on shared purpose and values explored in the building understanding stage.

This stage requires synthesis, analysis, and expert contribution. As our field of vision narrows, so too does our decision-making group. While building understanding sought diverse inputs, shaping choices prioritises decision-making mandate and relevant expertise. With clear criteria and expert input, this stage should produce a suite of meaningful options.

Tips for shaping choices

- Reduce the number of inputs and stakeholders at this stage in the process. Too many people will create noise without adding value.
- Focus on where views and opinions converge to build a shared criteria model for evaluating options.
- Seek independent analysis and advice in shaping up potential options.
- Use reference class data, case studies, and evidence-based recommendations to shape the options.

Decision stage 3: Make decisions

When there is a shared understanding of the decision to be made, agreement on evaluation criteria, and clear choices to consider, it's time to decide. These conversations will be calm if the previous two stages have been fully completed. If there is lingering conflict or confusion, go back and tackle any unresolved issues around the decision criteria or purpose. Proceeding without this commitment is asking for trouble.

In this decision stage, the goal is to commit to action. Participants agree on the next steps toward implementation – which might be intangible outcomes such as a policy or set of strategic priorities, or tangible outcomes such as committing funding, hiring staff, or kicking off a new project.

Tips for making decisions

- Reduce the number of people in the decision process even further so that only those who must approve the decision are actively involved.
- Don't decide too much at once. Make a minimum viable choice, then adapt and stay flexible as things develop and assumptions are tested in the real world.
- Do not rush to complete this stage if there is lingering unrest about the decision's criteria or purpose. Go back.

Decision non-linearity and productive disagreement

While each decision stage generally follows the other, the process will rarely be perfectly linear. Often, new information or changes in context require us to loop back.

If each stage includes the right stakeholders, decision-making will be easier, faster, and calmer – but that doesn't mean everybody will be enthusiastic about the result.

Remember, alignment is about productive disagreement. Democracy is about compromise, not conquering. It is okay for decision-makers to feel mildly but equally aggrieved by a decision, provided they are committed to its implementation.

FAIR INTENT

Every decision process is influenced by subjective values. The more participants involved and the more complex the issues, the greater the influence of our biases and value judgements.

The best local government leaders are aware of their own subjectivity and committed to operating with integrity. Fair intent in local government decisions includes meaningful engagement and managing bias.

Meaningful engagement

In local government, only those with the time to engage, skills to participate, and trust in the system are easily heard. The most vulnerable voices in our community, often the same people who are most affected by Council decisions over time, tend to be the quietest. Don't confuse the loudest voices with the most representative.

Engagement is not an act of charity. It's a smart way to improve decision quality. Diverse and meaningful engagement increases the odds of generating creative and compelling options and alternatives, even in complex situations.[65] Longitudinal research shows stakeholder participation lead to better decisions and new ideas, even in highly technical environments. A review of 239 cases of multi-stakeholder environmental decision-making in the United States over a 30-year period considered cost-effectiveness, contribution, and access to information and found a significant improvement in decision processes across the board.[66]

Engagement is good business – and doing it badly has serious consequences. You risk more than chicken owners and fountain lovers crying foul if you miss crucial opinions during the decision process.

65   Beierle, T. C., 2002.
66   Ibid.

You could inadvertently exacerbate inequality or cause future harm against a group you haven't heard from.

Ensuring everyone with mandate, enthusiasm, impact and/or interest has a meaningful participation opportunity is no easy feat. This is one reason decisions take so long in local government compared to business and other tiers of government.

This process must also include the people required to implement the decision's outcome. Without a sense of commitment and ownership, execution will fail to meet expectations.

> ## Engagement is not an act of charity; it's a smart move to improve decision quality.

Meaningful engagement doesn't mean a committee should make every decision or that every choice should be consulted on. It doesn't mean complex science, health, or engineering decisions should be made by laypeople. However, in a democratic institution, significant and impactful decisions should involve the right people and their opinions must be considered.

Tips for more informed decisions

- **Consider all affected parties:** Ensure everyone affected or interested in a decision or policy is considered in the consultation process. This includes not just the vocal majority but also minority groups and vulnerable populations.

- **Be proactive:** Go to stakeholders rather than expecting them to come to the Council. This might involve community visits, pop-up information sessions, or leveraging digital platforms for wider reach.

- **Identify missing voices:** Get in the habit of asking, 'Who haven't we talked to? Who have we missed?' This should be a standard part of every collaborative decision-making process to ensure comprehensive stakeholder engagement.

- **Use multiple engagement channels:** Different people prefer different methods of communication. Use surveys, public meetings, social media, focus groups, and other tools.

- **Provide feedback:** Establish mechanisms to inform stakeholders about how their input was used. This transparency builds trust and encourages future participation.

- **Train staff and Councillors:** Ensure all team members in the decision-making process understand the importance of stakeholder engagement and are skilled in facilitation.

Managing bias

When deciding what to do about my job, I was biased in ways I couldn't see. I had stories about motherhood shaped by popular culture and society. Good mothers, I thought, are there for their kids after school, have tins filled with baking, and put themselves last. I also had stories about success and what it was made of: money, marriage, and property. I was young, scared, and inexperienced, and my stories lacked nuance.

Everyone has a story in their head which shapes how they interpret information. That story is shaped by our experiences, the people we've spent time with, and the narrative we've crafted to explain those things. Over 200 potential biases affect our decisions, most of which are on autopilot.[67] We cannot escape bias but we can manage it.

---

67   Kahneman, D., 2011.

Make bias explicit

'Make explicit what is implicit in any decision you make.'

Annie Duke

Local government leaders are prone to all the same biases as everyone else, along with a few extras.[68] When you're closely connected to your community, you view the world through the lens of the people you talk to most and the problems you encounter regularly. When you're a subject matter expert, you see the world through the lens of your expertise. When your continued employment depends on re-election, you see the world through the lens of public opinion.

No matter what you do, you're biased. The good news is that strategic decisions aren't about becoming superhuman. Instead, they make bias, conflict, and assumptions explicit. Actively incorporating bias-busting tools into reports, workshops, and decision processes will improve the quality of decisions.

A bias-management model I use with Council groups is a tool called WRAP, pioneered by the Heath brothers in their book *Decisive*.[69] According to the Heath brothers, there are four main enemies of good decisions:

- *Narrow framing*: we think that what we see is all there is.
- *Confirmation bias*: we've got a solution in mind, so we see the problem through that lens.
- *Short-term emotions*: we're driven by excitement or fear and choose impulsively.

---

68 There is fascinating research about particular biases that apply to Councillors and Council managers. For example, a Danish experiment that sought to explain how performance information affects decision-making found that city Councillors will increase spending when performance is low (to avoid being blamed for continued poor performance) and also when it's high (to claim the credit) but not in areas with average performance, effectively penalising areas that function well. (Nielsen, P. A., & Baekgaard, M., 2015.)

69 Heath, C., & Heath, D., 2013.

- *Overconfidence:* we overestimate how complete our information is, how right we are, or how well things will turn out.

The Heath brothers suggest key steps to tackle each of these biases using the acronym WRAP:

- **W** is for widening your options. Because we're prone to narrow framing, we should expand our perspective. We can do that by 'frame storming', talking to others who see things differently, and seeking a full range of alternatives and options.

- **R** is for reality-testing assumptions. To prevent confirmation bias, we should try to prove ourselves wrong. We can do that by actively seeking disconfirming evidence, trying to take an 'outside view' by pretending to be someone else, or running small tests and experiments.

- **A** is for attaining distance before deciding. Aimed at tackling short-term emotions, this is the professional equivalent of your mother telling you to sleep on a big purchase before proceeding. Consider what you would advise a friend to do in the same situation and try to remove your personal investment.

- **P** is for preparing to be wrong, which seeks to counteract some of your overconfidence. Useful ways to do this include running a 'premortem', where you imagine all the things that might go wrong and plan how you would respond. You can also imagine multiple scenarios and outcomes and simulate failure.

Applying this model to your decision conversations and recording the discussion and results will bring more fairness to your decision processes, even if your bias is still present.

Chapter 15 summary

▯ Fair decisions are about process and intent.

▯ There are three stages in a strategic decision: building understanding, shaping choices, and making decisions.

▯ Fairness is about meaningful engagement and managing bias.

16

Focus

'I would not give a fig for the simplicity this side of complexity,
but I would give my life for the simplicity the other side
of complexity.'

Oliver Wendell Holmes

In the parable of Buridan's donkey, an equally hungry and thirsty donkey is placed exactly in the middle of a stack of hay and a pail of water. The donkey, unable to decide between the hay and the water, makes no decision and dies of hunger and thirst. This philosophical paradox, and variations of it, is named after the 14th-century French philosopher Jean Buridan, whose philosophy of moral determinism it satirises.

Many Council plans and strategies are written in the style of Buridan's donkey. They riff on the same four community outcomes or goals (economy, environment, society, and culture) and include a long wish list of objectives. There is no telling which outcomes or objectives are more important than the others. This might feel like diplomacy, political agreeableness, or even equity. But mostly, it's unclear and unhelpful.

Unless the relative importance of these outcomes is made clear, consistent decisions about budget allocations, project priorities, organisational design, learning and development programmes, relationship-building, fundraising, lobbying and advocacy, or recruitment strategies cannot be made.

By failing to make priority distinctions, local government leaders push judgement calls and decisions down to managers and frontline staff. Staff are forced to make ad hoc choices about how to spend their time, money, and energy with no strategic guidance. The chance of those decisions aligning neatly and effectively to shape the community in the way the Council wants is slim.

The hardest part of your leadership will not be deciding what to do: it will be deciding what *not* to do, who to let down, and which worthy cause to leave wanting. The hardest moments of your leadership will be the great ideas you don't pursue, the beneficial projects you don't fund, and the stakeholders you can't partner with. There is no escaping it. This is your job. Trade-offs are easy when they involve choosing between right and wrong – any idiot can do that. Choosing between right and right is hard, especially when no objectively correct answer exists.

Your leadership effectiveness will be determined by how clear your collective focus is. The clearer you are, the easier it will be for everyone to do their job, and the more likely you are to deliver on the most important goals and aspirations you hold for your community.

Focus isn't easy. Simplicity, at least the kind worth having, is on the other side of complexity. But your decisions will improve *because* you waded through frustration, disagreement, and conflict to get there, not in spite of it.

Three components of a strategic decision

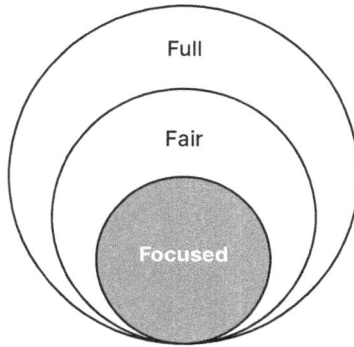

FOCUSED PERFORMANCE

Focus is a 'how' job. It asks for clear decisions about the criteria you'll use for choices to be made at the 'what' level. In strategic decisions, the focus is on clarifying *principles* and *priorities*.

Principles are rules or values. They determine the approach the Council will take to its work.

Priorities are specific focus areas or outcomes. They provide an applicable reference to determine which actions are most important.

Managers and staff use both criteria to make operational decisions. When criteria are clear, operational decisions will align with the Council's overall direction, driving performance.[70]

Priorities shape actions

Many leaders resist articulating and communicating their priorities, fearing the worst. The fear of non-compliance or public push-back is strong in a highly regulated and visible environment. The good news

---

70   Vandersmissen, L., & George, B., 2023.

is that priorities do not exclude necessities. Everything that needs to happen – legislative requirements, core business, etc. – still will.

We don't set priorities to exclude actions. We set priorities to enhance actions. A complex, multi-service organisation like a Council will always have dozens of competing activities and service lines. Once you set and communicate a priority, the delivery of those services changes.

> ## We don't set priorities to exclude actions. We set priorities to enhance actions.

If customer service comes first, that doesn't mean parking officers no longer hand out fines – but they might do so differently or change the grounds for appeal. It doesn't mean potholes don't get patched – but it might change the contractors' KPIs.

You also open the door to innovation. It's easier to name five white things in a fridge than five white things. Narrowing your field of vision doesn't constrain or disempower your managers and teams – it promotes innovation that produces better outcomes. Decision criteria in the form of principles and priorities are a performance aid, and they enable responsiveness in the face of changing conditions. Consider the following case study.

Example: Coast City Park redevelopment

Coast City Council plans to redevelop a large waterfront park. The park is a central feature of the city, popular for recreational activities, but its facilities are outdated, and parts are underutilised.

Decision Stage 1: Build understanding

The Council begins by building understanding. To gather diverse perspectives, it organises community forums, surveys, and focus groups, which are attended by both Councillors and Council managers.

Local residents, business owners, environmental groups, and park users share their views. Some want more playgrounds and sports facilities; others want more conservation and tranquillity. Council officers present the key findings and challenges to Council, who agree to establish a Future Park Working Group for the next decision phase. This group includes Councillors, Council officers, and key local stakeholders such as the chamber of commerce, environmental groups, Indigenous representatives, sporting groups, and state government.

Decision Stage 2: Shape choices

The Future Parks Working Group convenes to shape choices. They synthesise the consultation data and identify common themes before agreeing on three strategic priorities: environmental sustainability, community vibrancy, and modern facilities. These priorities are reported to the Council's next meeting, with a recommendation to proceed to tender for expert analysis and initial concept development. Council adopts this recommendation.

To refine their options, Council officers gather data. They analyse the park's current usage patterns, demographic trends, and population projections. They commission an environmental impact assessment and an economic analysis. After reviewing this data, the Working Group goes to tender and appoints a consulting firm to develop initial concepts.

The planners return six options. The Working Group meets to discuss them – but the meeting is tense. The majority of the group feels overwhelmed and dissatisfied. The options are more expensive than expected and look space-age compared to the current environment. Children's play areas have been reduced, and the furniture looks like sculpture art. Quiet accusations begin to circulate, blaming the Council and the planners for failing to meet the brief.

After a challenging meeting, the Working Group agrees to report back to the Council with their thoughts and recommendations. After some discussion, the Council adopts the Working Group's recommendations:

- **An update to strategic criteria.** The options developed by the planners are expensive, trendy, and over-specified. After the initial shock, the Working Group realised the consultants had delivered on the brief – but Council's criteria weren't quite right.

The Working Group suggests changing the 'Modern Facilities' priority to 'Future-proofed Spaces' to develop more lower-maintenance and multi-purpose spaces with inbuilt flexibility. They also suggest changing from 'Community Vibrancy' to 'Friendly and Fun' to encourage more child-friendly spaces and areas for social and cultural activities.

▪ **A second round of initial options.** Given that the first round of options was unsuitable, the Working Group requested funding for a second round of initial options based on the updated criteria.

The second round of options is received much more favourably, and the Working Group has a fun and high-energy meeting to discuss them. They evaluate the options according to cost, environmental impact, and community benefit, narrow them down to three viable concepts, and prepare a report to the Council. The Council resolves to run a short community engagement campaign to get feedback on the concepts from the community, including an online vote.

Decision Stage 3: Make decisions

Finally, the Council enters the decision-making stage. The Working Group reviews the three plans, considering the previously established criteria and the community vote results.

They select the top option and commit to the next steps: securing funding, scheduling construction, and maintaining open communication with the community throughout.

One year on

The redevelopment project faces challenges. Unforeseen environmental regulations delay construction, and initial costs exceed estimates.

When the regulatory change was announced, the Working Group reconvened to review the park's design changes. Despite the new rules and compliance complications, the Group quickly select a new preferred option. The constraints had changed, but their criteria remained the same. These updates were quickly and clearly communicated to Council and the community.

This example speaks to the importance of a fair decision process and focused decision criteria. A decision's context will always change, but criteria will provide clarity and consistency in any circumstance.

FOCUS HACKS

Setting priorities is more of an art than a science. Decision-makers need a deep understanding of context, views, and perspectives, and a shared vision for the future. This information will be used to agree on your strategic priorities, and no one else can tell you what matters the most to your community. This is local democracy.

Despite this, three useful hacks for strategic focus will work for all Councils: acknowledging constraints, weighting criteria, and evaluating collaboratively.

Hack 1: Practical realism

Begin from a place of realism. Your resources are scarce, and scarcity requires specialisation. There is no world where your Council can do everything. The only choice you have is whether to make trade-offs with intention, or by default.

Strategic Councils are explicit about their trade-offs. They acknowledge that while their aspirations are unlimited, their capabilities and resources are limited, so focus will be required.

Hack 2: Weighted criteria

Don't be like Buridan's donkey. Instead, agree the relative importance of your priorities and principles. Various methods, ranging from simple ranking to more complex analyses, can be used to determine the relative priority of top issues.

My preferred approach is based loosely on the Investment Logic Mapping methodology of 'problem statement' weighting. This method is popular with my clients, and remarkably effective. I call it the $100 Game.

The $100 Game

The premise of the $100 Game is to assess the relative priority of your high-priority issues.

The rules of the game are:

- You only have $100 to spend. This represents the finite amount of energy, bandwidth, and attention (not to mention resources) available.
- You cannot divide the $100 perfectly equally – i.e. $33 across three, or $25 across four.
- If you award something $10 or less, consider removing it.
- The resulting dollar allocation provides the weighted decision criteria.

For example, the top three priorities in your Council plan over the next four years might be: supporting local business, making the community safer, and greening the city. You can weight these priorities using the $100 game. Supporting local businesses might get $50 (a 50% weighting), making the community safer $30 (a 30% weighting), and greening the city $20 (a 20% weighting).

Weighted decision criteria make it significantly easier to make aligned operational decisions such as which projects to greenlight, which working groups to join, which Ministers to build relationships with, and which skills to hire for.

Hack 3: Collaborative evaluation

When local government leaders agree on criteria, decisions are about applying the rules, not debating the details. Instead of trying to be right, strategic local government leaders, like the Working Group in the Coast City Park example, spend their time and energy clarifying and applying their decision criteria.

Leaders can use a Multi-Criteria Decision-Analysis (MCDA) rubric, like those used to assess tender responses, to make complex decisions. Conversations in these collaborative evaluation sessions elevate from project details to strategic alignment.

Example: Council project prioritisation

Consider the following example of projects being scored for alignment with Council's top three priorities. Each project is scored from 0 to 3; 0 is low alignment or contribution to the priority, and 3 is very high alignment or contribution.

Key project	Supporting local business (50%)	Making the community safer (30%)	Greening our city (20%)	Weighted score	Rank
Increased road maintenance funding	1 (0.5)	1 (0.3)	0 (0)	0.8	5
City Development Plan review	2 (1)	2 (0.6)	2 (0.4)	2	1
Childcare centre strategy	1 (0.5)	1 (0.3)	1 (0.2)	1	4
Tourism campaign 'Live and Work in Our Town'	3 (1.5)	0 (0)	0 (0)	1.5	3
Urban streetlighting project	2 (1)	3 (0.9)	0 (0)	1.9	2

I have used this simple and powerful process hundreds of times and with dozens of Councils for everything from organisational plans to 10-year budgeting, and it has never failed to produce alignment.

This process makes it possible to be right and still not get your way. You can compromise with dignity if your preferred option is not the first choice. If the ranking feels incorrect to many people in the room, your priority weightings might be off. When this happens, take another look at the criteria – not the choices.

Chapter 16 summary

- Focus improves decision performance by elevating conversations and driving alignment.
- Focus is needed to bridge the gap between our aspirations and resources.
- Weighted decision criteria enable consistent and robust evaluation.
- Applying decision criteria in a collaborative setting leads to decisions that stick.

17

Decisions in practice

Strategic decisions are difficult to make. There's no right answer, no way of knowing how the alternative would have worked out, and the consequences are real and important. Local government has a unique set of circumstances that complicate these decisions.

OCCUPATIONAL HAZARDS

In *From Strategy to Action*[71], I explain the 'Layer of Crazy' – three components of a complex and contested government operating environment. In local government, these three factors – transparency, democracy, and bureaucracy – can feel like a straitjacket.

Transparency

All tiers of government encourage and attract scrutiny from the media and the public. In local government, decisions are made in public, with the public, or both, and the full decision process is

---

71   McKay, A., 2019.

captured for the media and the community to dissect and analyse well into the future.

The intensity of this transparency is more than most government departments could fathom. Councils are a major news source for their local paper and a hot discussion topic on social media, especially in rural and provincial areas. Councils attract attention for even the most minor issues or concerns. Major projects are scrutinised at every angle, with locals suddenly becoming experts on roads, construction, or urban planting and keen to protest or criticise even the most innocuous Council choices.

Democracy

Democracy requires consultation and engagement, which takes time. This engagement occurs in a political environment of near-constant job insecurity, where Councillors' mandate to represent their communities is regularly contested and challenged.

In Councils with ward-based representation, re-election can depend on whether a Councillor has furthered the interests of people living in just a few streets.

Community engagement, citizen participation, and deliberative democracy are worthy ideals – but they're not always helpful and are rarely fast. Citizen participation and community engagement on even basic topics tend to serve people with sufficient time to participate or special interests to protect.[72]

Politicians have little expertise in the areas they govern or in governance itself. Many Councillors are well-intentioned, self-employed, or semi-retired locals who want to contribute. It is rare, almost unheard of, for a Councillor to have had previous experience governing an organisation with dozens of distinct service lines, infrastructure worth hundreds of millions, and decisions that will impact multiple generations.

---

72 OECD, 2019.

Bureaucracy

All this transparency and democracy takes time and requires processes, policies, systems, committees, reports, meetings, checks, and balances to administer. Australia and New Zealand are two of the least corrupt democracies in the world, and trustworthiness requires a lot of paperwork.

The laws surrounding local government decisions are frustratingly prescriptive, leaving little room for adaptive planning and the ambiguity inherent in public policy.

Regulatory, compliance, and accountability burdens on local government are high, especially compared to state and federal governments. Infrastructure planning, performance reporting, disclosure, and financial management obligations create a tightly regulated environment. Councils are expected to minutely predict the costs and tasks of all their service lines years in advance – an impossible feat not required of the spheres of government who enforce the requirement. Any grants or funding transfers require additional reporting and accountability, and the rules surrounding Council meetings, workshops, elections, representation, and decisions are tightly governed.

DECISION INTERVENTIONS

The Layer of Crazy threatens to derail strategic decisions. The best way to overcome these factors is to have clear systems, frameworks, and policies that make it easy to do the right thing. The quality of your decision process will determine the quality of your decisions. You can enable quality decision processes by developing a decision framework and policy, writing better reports, holding better meetings and workshops, debriefing all significant decisions, shortening feedback loops, engaging earlier, and using the right strategic planning tools for the job.

Enable quality with a strategic decision framework

When we implement systems to counteract bias, widen our perspective, and test our thinking, we design decision environments that counter our inadequacies as flawed, fallible humans. Use tools like WRAP and the Right Decision Model, and develop a Strategic Decisions Policy, to bring consistency and integrity to your Council's process.

Three questions to develop a policy for your strategic decision process

Q: What constitutes a strategic decision?
Make the criteria for strategic decisions clear ahead of time. To distinguish between operational and strategic decisions, you might consider variables like horizon, significance, cost, values, uncertainty, and payoff periods.

Q: What steps must be taken when making a strategic decision?
Outline the mandatory steps at each stage of a strategic decision process, from building understanding to making decisions.

Q: What orders of strategic magnitude are there?
Consider categorising decisions according to their relative significance and outline who will be involved and what will be needed for a proportionate process.

For example:

- A Level 1 strategic decision might have a horizon of less than 10 years, a financial impact of less than $0.5 million, and/or low to moderate potential permanence. It might need regular updates from officers to Councillors at each stage of the decision process – building understanding, shaping choices, and making decisions.
- A Level 2 strategic decision might have a horizon of 10 to 20 years, a financial impact of $0.5 to $5 million, and/or moderate potential permanence. It might require Councillor

involvement in the 'shaping choices' phase – a workshop, indicative business case, or issues and options report.

- A Level 3 strategic decision might have a horizon of 20+ years, a financial impact of over $5 million, and/or moderate to high potential permanence. It might need Councillor and community involvement, including multiple workshops and rounds of consultation.

Your policy's specifics can be tailored to your Council, and the details are less important than the consistency and integrity of the process.

Write great reports

Council reports are often long, technical, and incomplete. Without trust and certainty, subject matter experts will try to shield their work from criticism with impenetrable jargon and far too much detail. Council officers should only provide the Council with recommendations and reports that enable strategic decision-making.

Invest in the report-writing skills of your staff to enable clarity, brevity and usefulness in Council papers.

Tips for improving report writing

- Link to the big picture: demonstrate how this connects to Council's long-term goals.
- Provide true options: present genuine alternatives rather than just the preferred option.
- Get real about risk: highlight potential risks associated with each option.
- Admit uncertainty: acknowledge the limitations of available information.
- Show your workings: clearly outline the rationale and evidence behind your recommendations and be honest about assumptions.

Hold better meetings and workshops

Effective meetings and workshops are essential for making strategic decisions. Unfortunately, most meetings are too long, too formal, and become bogged down in operational matters. Make a habit of having your meetings observed and audited, with regular debriefs to discuss opportunities for improvement.

Tips for improving meeting quality

- Structured agendas: clearly defined objectives and agendas keep discussions focused.
- Facilitated discussions: skilled facilitators manage group dynamics and ensure all voices are heard.
- Inclusive participation: encourage input from all participants, not just the most vocal.
- Action-oriented outcomes: ensure that each meeting concludes with clear, actionable decisions.
- Quality questions: ask curious questions that serve the room, with the assumption of positive intent.

Design early engagement decision processes

Councillors and stakeholders should be involved in the scoping phase of high-impact community decisions. Early engagement helps build consensus from the start, increasing the likelihood of successful implementation and Council and community support.

Tips for bringing in stakeholders earlier

- Publish a 'workshop schedule' months in advance for Councillors so they can plan for attendance at policy review and strategic planning conversations.
- Use ongoing stakeholder engagement methods such as surveys, town hall meetings, focus groups, and online forums to stay connected and access real-time insights.

Expand your strategic planning toolkit

Different facilitation and strategic planning methods strengthen or weaken the impacts of bias, group dynamics, and constraints on strategic decisions, affecting the outcome. Use the right tool for the job and prioritise the development of facilitation skills among your leaders.

Tips for selecting your strategic planning tool

- Creative approaches like offsite workshops and strategy retreats encourage generative thinking and help to expand perspective.
- Tangible strategy tools like SWOT analyses, balanced scorecards, and performance planning encourage operational thinking and help to narrow focus.
- Role-playing, team-building, and visual strategy mapping can help decision-makers see the benefits of collaboration.

Debrief all significant decisions

All significant decisions should be evaluated or debriefed. This process involves reviewing what went well, what didn't, and what can be improved for future decisions. This practice helps to build a culture of continuous improvement and accountability.

Tips for debriefing

- Encourage Councillors to schedule 'Councillor-only' debriefs after each Council meeting.
- Debriefs should discuss the meeting process and quality, not just the content of the discussion.

Create useful feedback loops

Using tools like the Right Decision Model and adhering to a consistent strategic decision process will improve your decisions. But that doesn't mean abandoning measurement entirely.

Outcome-based evaluation (OBE) is critical for measuring the impact of operational decisions. It tracks metrics on goal achievement, completion times, financial targets, and behaviour changes. OBE metrics focus on measurable results that indicate whether a decision addressed the problem it was intended to solve. This is appropriate for operational decisions, but measuring outcomes for strategic decisions is more difficult. As a compromise, we can report on intermediate outcomes (or 'leading indicators') as a proxy for progress. This allows us to shorten the potential feedback loop from decades to months or years.

Tips for shortening feedback loops

- Report on intermediate outcomes (or 'leading indicators') as a proxy for progress.
- The best short-term feedback loops will consider variables that are *necessary*, but not *sufficient* for success.

Examples: Shortening feedback loops with intermediate indicators

Example 1: Urban greening initiative

- **Context:** An urban greening initiative aimed at increasing green spaces and improving air quality in the city.
- **Long-term outcome:** Improved air quality and enhanced urban biodiversity.
- **Intermediate indicator:** Changes in local temperature and humidity levels in newly greened areas.

▪ **Explanation:** The Council can monitor progress by immediate environmental impacts that are necessary, but not sufficient, for achieving long-term air quality improvement.

Example 2: Local economic development plan

▪ **Context:** A local economic development plan focused on boosting small business growth and employment rates.

▪ **Long-term outcomes:** Increased employment rates and a thriving local economy.

▪ **Intermediate indicators:** The number of new business registrations in the area.

▪ **Explanation:** New business openings are a proxy indicator for increased employment and economic growth and signify increased confidence in the area.

Chapter 17 summary

▪ The 'Layer of Crazy' – transparency, democracy, and bureaucracy – make local government decisions particularly difficult.

▪ Practical interventions to improve decisions include instituting a decision policy, improving reports and meetings, debriefing decisions, designing for earlier engagement, using diverse strategic planning tools, and shortening feedback loops.

Decisions in summary

▌ Strategic decisions are more complex and ambiguous than operational decisions and require a different skillset.

▌ Strategic decisions drive clarity, alignment, and results across the organisation and community.

▌ Accuracy is difficult or impossible to attain for strategic decisions. This makes the process more important than the outcome.

▌ Strategic decisions should be **full**, **fair**, and **focused**.
  ▌ Full decisions are informed by asking the right questions.
  ▌ Fair decisions are a product of process and intent.
  ▌ Focused decisions need applied criteria.

▌ There are three stages of a decision process: building understanding, shaping choices, and making decisions.

▌ Practical interventions to support the decision shift include:
  ▌ Embedding tools such as the Right Decision Model and WRAP to support fairness and fullness.
  ▌ Creating clear systems, policies, and processes, including a strategic decisions policy.
  ▌ Using a range of facilitation tools according to the desired outcome.
  ▌ Improving reports and meetings with clarity, brevity, and relevance.
  ▌ Engaging with stakeholders earlier in the decision process.
  ▌ Shortening feedback loops with intermediate indicators.

STRATEGIC
MANAGEMENT

18

From experts to enablers

'A bad system will beat a good person every time.'
W. Edwards Deming

Some years ago, I worked with a large Council that created a new directorate for community development. They used to have many people on the ground delivering services, but decided to shift to a 'centre of excellence'. Instead of running programmes directly, the Council would broker, connect, and fund community-led initiatives.

It was a great model. If it worked, it would reduce the Council's workload, build trust and connection in the community, and improve the quality of neighbourhood services.

But they were almost completely ineffective for the first few years of operation – very little funding was distributed, and few programmes got off the ground. It wasn't the strategy that was the problem. They had a focused set of priorities, a robust operating model, capable people, and adequate funding. Called in to investigate, I soon stumbled across a barrier … almost by accident.

As a supplier to this Council, I had to register with their best-in-class procurement and financial management system. The Council considered this system a raging success. A year after implementation, they proudly reported that thanks to the new software, they'd reduced the Corporate Services cost base and implemented a wide range of controls to reduce risk.

This sounds great – until you're one of the community groups that want to partner with the community development team. To get through the first screen of the procurement platform, you need a formal constitution, charitable status, and $2 million in public liability insurance. Most community groups were being pushed out at the first hurdle. The Council's internal systems directly opposed their service delivery goals.

In this situation, the finance, risk, and procurement teams hadn't done anything wrong – they were doing all the right, best-practice things. However, when supporting communities in shaping their futures, their decisions were way out of step.

Making change happen in local government is already difficult enough. If the way we do business directly undermines our goals and intentions, it's near impossible. Strategic local government management aligns every aspect of the Council's operations with big-picture goals. The most powerful way to do this is by focusing on the quality of organisational systems.

THE PARADOX OF LEADERSHIP

The paradox of leadership is that the more you progress in your career, the further you move away from the source of your original value.[73] For Council managers, that means letting go of technical

---

73   McKeown, G., 2014.

details and subject matter expertise in favour of enterprise performance and systems design.

This is not an intuitive shift to make, nor one that is universally rewarded. Many employers and organisations demand a strategic outlook on the one hand and measure performance on short-term, department-level KPIs on the other.

Moving from operational management to strategic management is a game-changer for organisational performance. Strategic management ensures that organisational resources are allocated and organised in alignment with the Councillors' goals and priorities.

The design of your organisation determines whether the Council's goals and aspirations will sink or swim. Strategic management aligns organisational design with strategic direction.

> **Strategic management aligns organisational design with strategic direction.**

In this section

In this section, we'll consider:

- The hierarchy of organisational needs.
- Why best fit is more important than best practice.
- How to design enabling environments.

THE HIERARCHY OF ORGANISATIONAL NEEDS

You might be familiar with Maslow's Hierarchy of Needs, a psychological theory proposed by Abraham Maslow in 1943. It is often depicted as a pyramid with five levels of human needs, arranged in priority order from the most basic to the most complex.

Maslow's Hierarchy of Needs

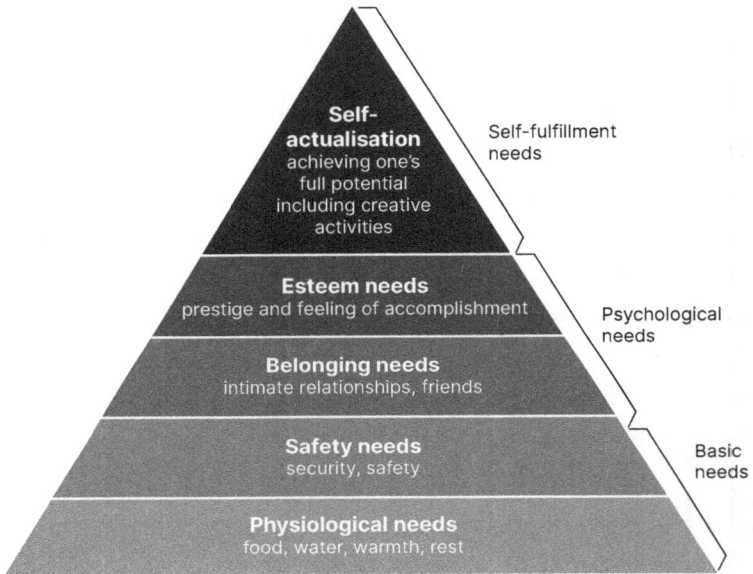

The basic idea is that not all human needs are created equally. We have fundamental needs (food, shelter, safety) that must be met before we think about the meaning of life.

Some years ago, working with a government agency that restructured its staff multiple times a year, I developed the McKay Hierarchy of Organisational Needs.

The idea is the same as Maslow's: not all organisational needs are created equally. Before we worry about the structure of our teams or start having conversations about 'changing the culture', we need to ensure basic needs are met. The foundation needs of any organisation are strategy and systems.

McKay's Hierarchy of Organisational Needs

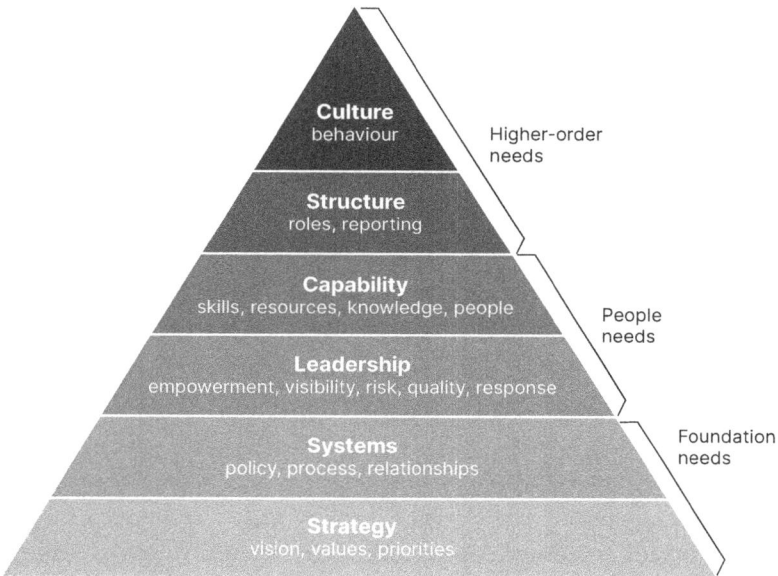

Strategy

Unless you have clarity on what you're about, where you're heading, and what people should focus on, it's extremely difficult for your people to use their time and energy wisely. Strategy determines the purpose of the organisation and shapes all the choices thereafter. Without it, your organisation will be disjointed and ineffective.

Systems

Unless organisations have the policies, processes, and relationships to make their strategy a reality, we're setting people up to fail. When delegations, financial rules, policies, customer service, or IT systems get in the way, progress lasts as long as our motivation does. Our goals are born in the boardroom but die in the backroom, so get that sorted before you worry about who's doing what. Make it easy for them to do the right thing.

> ## Our goals are born in the boardroom but die in the backroom.

* * *

Once foundational needs are met, leaders can consider the other parts of the organisation that require attention. Here's a brief overview of what to consider at each level.

Leadership

Performance comes from the top. Senior leaders must model desired behaviours if they want others to follow suit. These behaviours might include empowering people to do a great job, focusing on the responsibilities at their pay grade and delegating the rest, managing strategic risk, setting clear bottom lines, seeing the big picture, and responding quickly and effectively to crises. Invest in your leaders' strategic capacity, and watch the tide begin to turn.

Capability

When you know what you're doing, you've created an environment that makes it easy to do the right thing, and you're leading from the front, strategic managers can consider the skills and resources needed to drive progress. Capability isn't about off-the-shelf training or buying in talent from other organisations – it's about the institutional knowledge, skills, and resources you need to close the gap between the current state and future goals.

Structure

When you've got your other ducks in a row, consider structuring lines of responsibility, communication, and accountability. Do not focus solely on *organisational* structure. Instead, think about *decision* structure.

Performance isn't about where people sit; it's about the quality of their choices. Successful organisations make and execute good decisions, so work out what those decisions are, which ones are the most important, and the fastest and easiest ways to make them.

> Performance isn't about where people sit; it's about the quality of their choices.

Culture

Culture is in vogue and blamed for a full spectrum of ills at work, but culture is a higher-order need and mostly an output. It's less something that can be tweaked and more a daily reflection of everything that comes before it. People come to work to do a good job, and when that is made easy and possible (because foundational needs are taken care of), they generally do.

Diagnose your needs

When looking for ways to improve organisational performance, work through the hierarchy of needs to find opportunities for improvement.

Try asking questions like:

- Do we know where we want to be in five years?
- Are our top three priorities clear?
- Is it easy to do good work here?

- Do our business rules and systems support progress?
- Are our leaders focused on the right things?
- Do we have the skills and capabilities we need to achieve our goals?
- Are decisions made in the right place and by the right people?

Chapter 18 summary

- Strategic management is not an intuitive or universally rewarded leadership practice.

- Strategic management aligns organisational design with strategic direction.

- There is a hierarchy of organisational needs, with strategy and systems at the foundation.

19

Organisational performance

*A system's performance depends on how the parts fit,
not how they act taken separately.'*

Dr Russell Ackoff[74]

Strategic management in local government aligns the Council's functions and resources with its strategic direction. This means prioritising 'best fit' over 'best practice'. In our community development example, the Council had implemented best-practice financial management – but the parts didn't fit together.

Strategic management aligns your work with the overall direction of the Council, but it is only partially determined by how well you and your team carry out your responsibilities. The real test of your work is how well you integrate with other parts of the organisation in service of the broader goal.

---

74   Brant, S., 2010, 1994.

Here are a few examples:

▌ Suppose you are the Accounting Manager or Chief Financial Officer. In that case, your job is not to do best-practice accounting – it's to ensure the Council's financial management and accounting practices align with its long-term direction.

▌ Suppose you are the Policy Manager or Director of Community Services. In that case, your job is not to develop best-practice policy but to ensure the Council's policy and governance frameworks serve its strategic objectives.

▌ Suppose you are the Roads Manager or Director of Infrastructure. In that case, your job is not to deliver best-practice infrastructure – it's to ensure the Council's infrastructure programme aligns with its big-picture goals.

* * *

A system has three main components: its purpose, its parts, and the interactions between parts. To change a system, there are three main options: change the purpose, the parts, or the interactions.

Changing the parts of a system (i.e. the person in each role or the department responsible for a piece of work) is the least effective way to change the results a system produces. The two most effective ways to create systems change are to change how the parts interact or to change the system's purpose. Strategic managers do both. They change how the parts interact by breaking down silos and designing enabling environments, and they tackle the system's purpose by pursuing relentless alignment.

Strategic managers do three critical things:

1. Break down silos.
2. Design enabling environments.
3. Pursue relentless alignment.

BREAK DOWN SILOS

I once had to halt a strategic improvement workshop after a group of three participants proudly presented their business change idea to the rest of the group: an enterprise project management office. They explained the potential benefits: more consistent and robust project planning, a cross-organisational view, clearer expectations around approvals and funding, and more transparent accountability for performance.

The idea was great, and the room was enthusiastic. The only problem was: this Council already *had* an enterprise project management office. Nobody knew it existed.

I've partnered with several Councils where I seem to know more about the organisation than those working there. Everyone is so busy trying to do a good job they don't look up to see what anyone else is doing. Silos are the antithesis of systems.

Silos are the antithesis of systems.

When Councils operate in silos:

- Patchy and ineffective communication creates misunderstandings and delays.
- Different departments work towards different, sometimes conflicting, goals.
- Redundant processes and tasks drain time and budget without adding value.
- Critical risks are overlooked until too late, increasing project failure rates.
- Limited knowledge-sharing means missed improvement opportunities.

▌ Insufficient collaboration stifles innovation and creative solutions.

▌ Duplicated effort leads to wasted resources and inefficiency.

▌ Service delivery and customer service become inconsistent.

Disjointed and misaligned change initiatives do more harm than good, driving fatigue and frustration. Strategic management requires keeping tabs on who's doing what and keeping things pointing in the same direction.

Bringing people together and breaking down silos isn't an easy job, but it's one worth doing. The more smoothly information flows between different parts of your organisation, and the better aligned your teams are, the faster and easier strategic progress becomes.

Tips for breaking down silos

▌ Maintain an enterprise register of policy and business change projects for regular review and discussion by the executive leadership team.

▌ Encourage cross-functional teams and collaborative projects to promote a more integrated approach to problem-solving and innovation.

▌ Identify areas where information gets 'stuck' for core processes like planning, customer service, and consenting and work on improving those flows.

▌ Bring people into organisational and business planning programmes from across different teams and seniority levels.

▌ Require cross-departmental consultation for all significant project planning, especially for corporate services, policy, and customer-facing functions.

▌ Hold regular Town Hall style showcases for visibility of key projects and work programmes.

DESIGN ENABLING ENVIRONMENTS

When I ask Council staff what's making it difficult to make progress on their most important pieces of work, there are three common answers:

▪ Councillors.

▪ The community.

▪ Internal systems.

There's not much you can do about the first two, but the third item is well within the remit of a strategic manager. Business rules, policies, processes, or platforms are often introduced to improve service quality or efficiency only to have the opposite effect. Whether it's procurement and finance, a Customer Request Management (CRM) system, business case templates, or project management methodology, business systems have a bad reputation for making people's lives more difficult, slowing down workflows, and making it unnecessarily difficult to get anything done.

Our systems should facilitate work, making it easier to get things done. CRM platforms should make tracking the progress of service requests easier, not create an overwhelming administrative overhead. Business case templates should make investment decisions more robust and consistent, not stifle innovation.

When the right thing to do isn't the easiest thing to do – or, in some cases, is even the hardest thing to do! – it either doesn't get done, doesn't get done quickly, or gets done via a series of inconsistent and risky workarounds. The perverse incentives created by poorly aligned systems often create hidden risks inside organisations.

There are a range of reasons that Council work environments so often become disabling rather than enabling, including:

▪ *Risk-aversion* – The 'Layer of Crazy' (Chapter 17) drives risk-aversion in local government. The consequences of mistakes and errors are real and public, which often means the driver for policy change is to avoid harm or reduce risk rather than achieve goals or increase performance.

▪ *Over-specification* – What we focus on grows. Subject matter experts are biased toward overcomplication, and people tend to overstate the number of steps they take to complete a task. Steps, features, and options that sound good in theory are often onerous in practice.

▪ *Lack of internal consultation* – Policies, processes, and systems are often developed in isolation of the people who need to use, apply, and interact with them. This results in conflict, duplication, and a lack of usability.

▪ *Underinvestment in training and development* – Business change and technology projects are notorious for running over time and budget. Once implementation is reached, the patience and budget for training and development is often sparse. This slows down or threatens widespread adoption.

Tackling these behaviours is challenging and requires leadership commitment, but the results can be transformational for employee engagement and organisational performance.

Tips to design enabling environments

▪ Regularly review and streamline processes to eliminate unnecessary steps that add complexity without value.

▪ Empower employees to make decisions within their delegation and scope of responsibilities.

▪ Provide clear guidelines and frameworks within which employees can operate autonomously.

▪ Seek frequent feedback on the suitability and ease of policies and processes – and act quickly on the results.

- Allocate time and resources specifically for innovation, creativity, and business improvement sprints.
- Create the minimum viable policy, process, or system. Resist the temptation to over-specify or overcomplicate.
- Invest in learning and development for all business systems.
- Always 'greenfield' new processes and ask the question: 'What is the simplest and easiest way to get our desired outcome?'
- Remember to design for what you *do* want, rather than trying to prevent what you *don't* want.
- Engage users and stakeholders early, meaningfully, and often in your design.
- Test, test, and test again. Be willing to change your mind.

PURSUE RELENTLESS ALIGNMENT

Most departments and teams have a distorted perception of their work's purpose. Convinced of their work's inherent importance, they forget they are part of a broader system. Encouraging Council staff to realign existing work through the lens of a shared purpose can shift outcomes without requiring transformational change.

Consider these examples:

- Monitoring and compliance have no inherent value. They support public health, safety, or environmental protection goals. Ensuring monitoring teams are focused on delivering these outcomes rather than individual monitoring tasks could fundamentally shift how regulatory officers interact with customers. This drives improved customer satisfaction, increased compliance rates, and better health and environmental outcomes.

▌ Parks maintenance has no inherent value. It supports goals like improved amenity value and better access to recreation opportunities. When parks staff prioritise enhanced amenity value and recreation access over completing specific maintenance tasks, the shape and quality of open spaces shift for the better.

▌ Human resources have no inherent value. They support the development of Council staff who deliver high-quality services and outcomes to the community. When HR is aligned to this purpose and equipped to deliver on it, its approach to capability development, hiring, and performance transforms. This improves employee engagement, satisfaction, and fulfilment to produce better community outcomes.

Every part of the Council has a critical role to play in delivering the Council's broader goals, but this is easily forgotten in the constant march toward deadlines and compliance. Strategic management focuses on relentless alignment, which is where the gold lies.

Tips for creating alignment

▌ Regularly incorporate the Council's vision and strategic goals into corporate communications.

▌ Spend time with teams and leaders to meaningfully connect their work to the Council's vision and strategic objectives.

▌ Implement a cascading-goals framework where high-level strategic objectives are translated into specific, measurable goals for departments and individuals.

▌ Link individual performance to strategic progress. Include conversations about collaborative and shared goals in performance appraisals.

▌ Align rewards and recognition programs with strategic objectives to reinforce behaviours and outcomes that support shared goals.

- Workshop new projects and programmes with questions like:
  - 'How does this contribute to achieving the Council's strategic objectives?'
  - 'How can we make achieving the Council's big-picture goals easier, faster, or better?'
- Empower teams and individuals to make decisions within their remit that deliver on higher-order outcomes and intent over operational output.
- When selecting IT systems, project management frameworks, or policy approaches, prioritise collaborative capability and integration over feature richness.

Chapter 19 summary

- Strategic managers break down silos, design enabling environments, and pursue relentless alignment.

Local Legends:
A final summary

- Councils provide essential community infrastructure beyond basic utilities. Strategic local government leadership is crucial for leaving a powerful legacy.

- Strategy comprises three main components: the 'why', 'how', and 'what' levels. Many Councils struggle with a 'missing middle' in their strategy framework.

- There are important differences between strategies in the private and public sectors. Local government leaders create public value, which is more complex than generating profit.

- Councils operate at different levels of strategic capability, from lagging to legendary. Three strategic shifts will address local government's most common challenges: perspective, relationships, and decisions.

- Perspective is critical for local government leaders to make high-quality decisions. Perspective has three elements: horizon, significance, and context.

- Relationships between elected and executive leaders are critical for progress. Healthy relationships between governance and management in local government have three observable characteristics: reliance, role clarity, and respect.

- Strategic decisions are more complex and ambiguous than operational decisions and require a different skillset. They should be full, fair, and focused.

- Strategic management is required for an organisation to deliver on the Council's strategic priorities. It is about designing organisational systems that facilitate progress.

Conclusion

I'm from a lower working-class background, where many people were addicted to cigarettes. In childhood, I witnessed financial angst as we battled to make ends meet, but there were always cigarettes. This can be difficult for people who grew up in different circumstances to comprehend. Long-term poverty changes the incentives; there is no light at the end of the tunnel. It is not a brief adventure, like being a student or going backpacking. It is a whole life. If that money isn't spent on cigarettes, it will be absorbed immediately by something else.

When you're perpetually behind and always juggling, it is rational and sensible to seek short-term, intermittent pleasures with your money rather than delay gratification for a brighter day which might never come. Chronic poverty keeps people trapped in a short-term decision cycle.

Local government faces chronic poverty. In some ways, democracy has a scarcity mindset baked in. Election cycles drive short-term thinking – there's no point upsetting the public in service of a long-term good if you're voted out before you can see it through.

At a regulatory level, systemic disempowerment and underfunding embed this thinking – if you're never going to get what you need, why think 100 years out? The sector needs reform, resources, and respect to fully realise its potential for legacy leadership.

In the interim, here are the top five things you can work on inside your Council that will pay long-term dividends and build sustainable capability – in order of priority:

1. *Improve the relationship within and between governance and management.* Change moves at the speed of trust. The better this relationship functions, the more progress you'll be able to make.

2. *Get clear on your shared goals and values.* You agree on much more than you think. You won't be able to change the world in one Council term, but you can make decisions you're proud of. Put your values front and centre.

3. *Invest in Councillor development, from induction and beyond.* Long-term direction depends on the capability of elected members to think big-picture, form alliances, and own their strategic decision role.

4. *Use your meeting time more wisely (and write shorter reports).* Stop wasting time on trivialities. Your meeting time and attention span are sacred and scarce; treat them as such.

5. *Ask better questions – and with more respect.* Think beyond individual examples and citizen gripes and look at the big picture – trends, goals, etc.

The three strategic shifts outlined in this book can potentially transform your Council's impact. I've implemented these tried-and-tested methods in Councils of all types, sizes, and constraints on both sides of the Tasman. But you need the will of a dedicated Mayor and CEO/ General Manager who work well together to make it happen.

The work you do is important. It's meaningful, tangible, critical community support delivered in uncertain times. We need local government more than ever, and while the conditions may not be perfect, there is no sector quite like it. Keep doing what you're doing – we need you.

Thanks for reading.

Alicia McKay

Acknowledgements

Thank you to Michael Hanrahan and Anna Clemann at Publish Central for your patience in the face of my pedantry, and to Bernard Salt, Haydn Read, Clinton Jury, Paul Evans, and Bligh Grant for your keen eyes and kind words.

Thank you to the governance and leadership teams at Glen Eira City Council, City of Mitcham and Mildura Rural City Council for agreeing to have your stories told – and for trusting me to tell them.

Thank you to the Local Government Professionals Associations in New South Wales and Victoria for your support and excitement in helping me launch this book and for trusting me with your members and delegates at conferences, training and events.

A special thank you to Gavin Thomas and Ashburton District Council for hiring me as a keen graduate in 2010. My time at ADC ignited a spark for local government – a light that has burned brightly at times, dimmed at others, but never gone out.

Most importantly, thank you to all the Councillors and Council managers who have invited me into their Chambers and communities over the last 14 years. Being part of your stories has been a privilege and a pleasure.

My work with Councils has taken me places I would never have otherwise seen. Whether I'm sweating bullets in the outback, fighting for meeting rooms in the city, or learning from local librarians, I have treasured my time with each and every one of you.

I've tried 'real' government (eye roll, but if you know, you know), I've tried corporate, and just about everything in between, and I've gotta say, for better or worse: there's no place quite like local government.

AM

Appendix

Strategic audit

Here is a high-level assessment framework you can use to audit how strategic your Council is and identify areas for improvement.

Assessment criteria

The five assessment themes in this audit fall under two categories: strategic leadership and strategic management. Each theme assesses three headline indicators to provide an overall understanding of the strategic capability of your Council.

Rating scale

This diagnostic uses a five-point Likert scale for each criterion:

    1 = Never
    2 = Not very often
    3 = Some of the time
    4 = Most of the time
    5 = Always

Evaluation

Evaluate your total performance using the below guidance. Consider your score for each group and each theme when identifying what to work on next.

Audit questions

Theme	Criteria	Rating
Strategic leadership		
Perspective	The average payoff period of decisions made at the Council table is over 10 years.	
	Council and executive team meetings focus on strategically significant decisions and opportunities.	
	Risks and consequences are discussed at a multi-generational and multi-stakeholder level.	
	Perspective score	
Relationships	There is demonstrable collegiality and warmth between the elected and executive.	
	Councillors respectfully disagree in private and public forums without personal conflict and regularly reach consensus.	
	Executive managers give free and frank advice without fear or defensiveness.	
	Relationships score	
Decisions	The criteria and process for how to make a strategic decision is well understood by Councillors and officers. Councillors are involved in the scoping and design stage of significant decisions and policy reviews.	

Theme	Criteria	Rating
Decisions (cont.)	Council papers and reports are brief, clear, and focused on trends, options, and outcomes. All recommendations are clearly linked to strategic priorities, true options are provided, and relevant risks are detailed. Uncertainty is exposed and workings are shown.	
	Contentious decisions are accepted once made and not relitigated in Chambers or the media.	
	Decisions score	
Total score: Strategic leadership		
Strategic management		
Systems	Managers have the resources, support, and capabilities needed to deliver their work programme or there is a roadmap to address gaps.	
	Executive team meetings focus on enterprise-wide concerns, opportunities for collaboration, or removal of organisational barriers to performance.	
	Staff broadly agree with the statement that 'they are empowered to do their job'.	
	Systems score	
Alignment	The relative importance of medium-term and short-term priorities is clear across the organisation.	

Theme	Criteria	Rating
Alignment (cont.)	Departmental and individual performance objectives are linked to the achievement of broad strategic goals.	
	Core IT systems, project management frameworks, and policy approaches prioritise collaboration and integration.	
	Alignment score	
Total score: Strategic management		
TOTAL SCORE:		

Theme score:

3–5: Very low. Immediate action is required.

6–8: Low. Priority for change.

9–11: Moderate. Needs work.

12–14: High. Doing well.

15: Very high. Nailing it!

Total score:

15–27: Lagging. Very low strategic capability.

28–39: Overwhelmed. Low strategic capability.

40–50: Compliant. Moderate strategic capability.

51–63: Ambitious. High strategic capability.

64–75: Legendary. Very high strategic capability.

About the author

Alicia McKay is New Zealand's and Australia's leading expert on local government strategy and leadership. Alicia has worked with over 50 Councils in the last decade and is a trusted advisor to the sector.

Alicia is also the author of *From Strategy to Action: A guide to getting shit done in the public sector* and *You Don't Need An MBA: Leadership lessons that cut through the crap.*

Her influence extends beyond local government. Alicia has collaborated with a wide range of government agencies and corporate clients, offering support in strategic leadership development and organisational transformation. Her clients range from industry giants to small NGOs.

Alicia lives in Wellington, New Zealand, with her three children.

To learn more about Alicia, head to www.aliciamckay.co.nz.

References

Ansell, C., & Gash, A. (2008a). Collaborative Governance in Theory and Practice. *Journal of Public Administration Research and Theory: J-PART, 18*(4), 543-571. http://www.jstor.org/stable/25096384

Ansell, C., & Gash, A. (2008b). A Model of Collaborative Governance.

Beierle, T. C. (2002). The Quality of Stakeholder-Based Decisions. *Risk Analysis, 22*(4), 739-749. https://doi.org/10.1111/0272-4332.00065

Brant, S. (2010, 1994). *If Russ Ackoff had given a TED Talk*. https://www.youtube.com/watch?v=OqEeIG8aPPk

Cabinet, D. o. t. P. M. a. (2022). *Trust in Australian public services: 2022 Annual Report*. Australian Government Retrieved from https://www.pmc.gov.au/sites/default/files/resource/download/trust-aps-annual-report-2022.pdf

Caplan, B. (2007). *The Myth of the Rational Voter: Why Democracies Choose Bad Policies*. Princeton University Press.

Chrislip, D. D. L., Carl E. (1994). *Collaborative Leadership: How Citizens and Civic Leaders Can Make a Difference*. Jossey Bass.

Christensen, J., Dahlmann, C., Mathiasen, A., Moynihan, D., & Petersen, N. B. G. (2018). How Do Elected Officials Evaluate Performance? Goal Preferences, Governance Preferences, and the Process of Goal Reprioritization. *Journal of Public Administration Research and Theory*, 28, 197-211. https://doi.org/10.1093/jopart/muy001

Connelly, B. L., Crook, T. R., Combs, J. G., Ketchen, D. J., & Aguinis, H. (2018). Competence- and Integrity-Based Trust in Interorganizational Relationships: Which Matters More? *Journal of Management*, 44(3), 919-945. https://doi.org/10.1177/0149206315596813

Cookson, J. (2019). Local Government History and Localism. *Policy Quarterly*, 15(2), 19-24.

Covey, S. M. R. a. M., Rebecca R. (2006). *The Speed of Trust: The one thing that changes everything.* Free Press.

Douglas, M. (2006). *Local Government Structure and Efficiency: A report prepared for Local Government New Zealand.*

Downes, B. T. (1998). Catalytic Leadership: Strategies for an Interconnected World [Book review]. *The Social Science Journal*, 35, 657. https://link.gale.com/apps/doc/A53392170/AONE?u=anon~85f47393&sid=googleScholar&xid=1cd8deb1

Edelman. (2022). *Edelman Trust Barometer 2022.* https://www.edelman.com/sites/g/files/aatuss191/files/2022-01/2022%20Edelman%20Trust%20Barometer%20FINAL_Jan25.pdf

Ertel, C., & Solomon, L. K. (2014). *Moments of Impact: How to design strategic conversations that accelerate change.* Simon & Schuster.

European Public Service Union. (2019). *Public and Private Sector Efficiency.* https://www.epsu.org/sites/default/files/article/files/EN_EFFICIENCY%20for%20web.pdf

Future for Local Government Review Panel. (2023). *He piki tūranga, he piki kōtuku: The future for local government.* Wellington, New Zealand: Future for Local Government Review Panel

Gaddis, J. L. (2018). *On Grand Strategy*. Penguin Press.

George, B., & Desmidt, S. (2014). A State of Research on Strategic Management in the Public Sector: An Analysis of the Empirical Evidence. In (pp. 151-172).

George, B., Desmidt, S., Cools, E., & Prinzie, A. (2018). Cognitive styles, user acceptance and commitment to strategic plans in public organizations: an empirical analysis. *Public Management Review*, *20*(3), 340-359. https://doi.org/10.1080/14719037.2017.1285112

George, B., Walker, R. M., & Monster, J. (2019). Does Strategic Planning Improve Organizational Performance? A Meta-Analysis. *Public Administration Review*, *79*(6), 810-819. https://doi.org/10.1111/puar.13104

Grant, B. (2021). The Particular Applicability of Public Value Creation to Local Government. *International Journal of Public Administration*, *44*(10), 835-844. https://doi.org/10.1080/01900692.2021.1903497

Grimmelikhuijsen, S., Porumbescu, G., Hong, B., & Im, T. (2013). The Effect of Transparency on Trust in Government: A Cross-National Comparative Experiment. *Public Administration Review*, *73*(4), 575-586. https://doi.org/10.1111/puar.12047

Grimmelikhuijsen, S. G. (2010). Transparency of Public Decision-Making: Towards Trust in Local Government? *Policy & Internet*, *2*(1), 5-35. https://doi.org/10.2202/1944-2866.1024

Hansen, K. M., & Ejersbo, N. (2002). The relationship between politicians and administrators – a logic of disharmony. *Public Administration*, *80*(4), 733-750. https://doi.org/10.1111/1467-9299.00326

Heath, C., & Heath, D. (2013). *Decisive: How to make better choices in life and work*. Crown Currency.

Herbst, S. (1998). *Reading Public Opinion: How Political Actors View the Democratic Process*. The University of Chicago Press.

Kahneman, D. (2011). *Thinking, fast and slow*. Farrar, Straus and Giroux.

Krznaric, R. (2020). *The Good Ancestor A radical prescription for long-term thinking*. The Experiment.

Lencioni, P. M. (2002). *The Five Dysfunctions of a Team*. Jossey-Bass.

Lorenz-Spreen, P., Mønsted, B. M., Hövel, P., & Lehmann, S. (2019). Accelerating dynamics of collective attention. *Nature Communications*, *10*(1), 1759. https://doi.org/10.1038/s41467-019-09311-w

Macaskill, W. (2022). *What We Owe The Future: A million-year view*. Oneworld Publications.

McKay, A. (2019). *From Strategy to Action: A guide to getting shit done in the public sector*. Structured Conversations Limited.

McKay, A. (2021). *You Don't Need An MBA: Leadership lessons that cut through the crap*. Major Street Publishing.

McKeown, G. (2014). *Essentialism: The disciplined pursuit of less*. Virgin Books.

McSpadden, K. (2015). You Now Have a Shorter Attention Span Than a Goldfish. *TIME*. https://time.com/3858309/attention-spans-goldfish/

Moore, M. H. (1995). *Creating Public Value: Strategic management in government*. Harvard University Press.

Morse, R. (2008). Developing Public Leaders in an Age of Collaborative Governance. In (pp. 79-100).

Nielsen, P. A., & Baekgaard, M. (2015). Performance Information, Blame Avoidance, and Politicians' Attitudes to Spending and Reform: Evidence from an Experiment. *Journal of Public Administration Research and Theory*, *25*(2), 545-569. https://doi.org/10.1093/jopart/mut051

OECD. (2019a). *OECD Recommendation of the Council on Public Service Leadership and Capability*. https://web-archive.oecd.org/2019-07-17/526235-recommendation-on-public-service-leadership-and-capability-en.pdf

OECD. (2019b). *Public Value in Public Service Transformation: Working with Change*.

Olson, B. J., Parayitam, S., & Bao, Y. (2007). Strategic Decision Making: The Effects of Cognitive Diversity, Conflict, and Trust on Decision Outcomes. *Journal of Management*, *33*(2), 196-222. https://doi.org/10.1177/0149206306298657

Poister, T., Pitts, D., & Edwards, L. (2010). Strategic Management Research in the Public Sector: A Review, Synthesis, and Future Directions. *American Review of Public Administration – AMER REV PUBLIC ADM*, *40*, 522-545. https://doi.org/10.1177/0275074010370617

Premier of Victoria, H. J. A. M. (2023). *Reforms To Boost Confidence In Local Government*. Retrieved 14 March from https://www.premier.vic.gov.au/reforms-boost-confidence-local-government

PWC. (2022). *Local Government Culture Project Insights Report*. https://www.localgovernment.vic.gov.au/__data/assets/pdf_file/0019/186211/090522_FINAL-updated_LG-Culture-Project_Insights-Report.pdf

Ripple, W. J., Larsen, E. J., Renkin, R. A., & Smith, D. W. (2001). Trophic cascades among wolves, elk and aspen on Yellowstone National Park's northern range. *Biological Conservation*, *102*(3), 227-234. https://doi.org/10.1016/S0006-3207(01)00107-0

Samuel, H. (2012). Eiffel Tower worth £344 billion to French economy – or six Towers of London. *The Telegraph*. https://www.telegraph.co.uk/news/worldnews/europe/france/9492500/Eiffel-Tower-worth-344-billion-to-French-economy-or-six-Towers-of-London.html#:~:text=The%20Eiffel%20Tower%20has%20been,economy%2C%20a%20new%20study%20claims.&text=The%20venerable%20Paris%20landmark%20was,euros%20%20(%C2%A372%20billion).

Saxe, J. G. (1872). *The Blind Men and The Elephant*.

SGS Economics and Planning. (2022). *Local Government Productivity Report*. https://sgsep.com.au/projects/local-government-productivity-report

Simons, T. L., & Peterson, R. S. (2000). *Task conflict and relationship conflict in top management teams: The pivotal role of intragroup trust* [doi:10.1037/0021-9010.85.1.102]. American Psychological Association.

SPCA. *Debunking goldfish myths*. Retrieved 16 May from https://www.spca.nz/advice-and-welfare/article/debunking-goldfish-myths#:~:text=Myth%201%20%2D%20Goldfish%20Have%20a%203%2DSecond%2DMemory&text=However%2C%20the%20truth%20is%20quite,sense%20of%20time%20and%20routine.

Sullivan, H., Downe, J., Entwistle, T., & Sweeting, D. (2006). The three challenges of community leadership. *Local Government Studies*, *32*(4), 489-508. https://doi.org/10.1080/03003930600793136

Tour Eiffel. (2023). *When the Eiffel Tower was a subject of controversy*. Tour Eiffel. Retrieved 6 March 2023 from https://www.toureiffel.paris/en/news/history-and-culture/when-eiffel-tower-was-subject-controversy

Vandersmissen, L., & George, B. (2023). Strategic planning in public organizations: reviewing 35 years of research. *International Public Management Journal*, 1-26. https://doi.org/10.1080/10967494.2023.2271901

Vandersmissen, L., George, B., & Voets, J. (2024). Strategic planning and performance perceptions of managers and citizens: analysing multiple mediations. *Public Management Review*, *26*(2), 514-538. https://doi.org/10.1080/14719037.2022.2103172

Walgrave, S., Jansen, A., Sevenans, J., Soontjens, K., Pilet, J.-B., Brack, N., Varone, F., Helfer, L., Vliegenthart, R., Meer, T. v. d., Breunig, C., Bailer, S., Sheffer, L., & Loewen, P. J. (2023). Inaccurate Politicians: Elected Representatives' Estimations of Public Opinion in Four Countries. *The Journal of Politics*, *85*(1), 209-222. https://doi.org/10.1086/722042

www.ingramcontent.com/pod-product-compliance
Lightning Source LLC
Chambersburg PA
CBHW030504210326
41597CB00013B/792